Spotte

NATURE

Internet links

There are lots of fun websites where you can find out more about nature. We have created links to some of the best sites on the Usborne Quicklinks Website. To visit these sites, go to www.usborne-quicklinks.com and enter the keywords "spotters nature". Here are some of the things you can do on the internet:

❀ Keep an online nature diary
❀ Find out which flowers grow near your home
❀ Design a tree and find out how it would survive in different climates
❀ Play bird games and dissect a virtual owl pellet
❀ Watch video clips of bee dances

Internet safety

Usborne
Spotter's Guide to
NATURE

Christopher J. Humphries
Department of Botany, The Natural History Museum

Esmond Harris
Director of the Royal Forestry Society

Peter Holden
National Organizer of the Junior Section of the
Royal Society for the Protection of Birds

Anthony Wootton

Illustrated by Hilary Burn,
Annabel Milne, Peter Stebbing,
Trevor Boyer, Phil Weare

Consultants:
Richard Scott
Derek Patch, Director, Tree Advice Trust
Dr Margaret Rostron

Contents

6 How to use this book
10 When and where to spot
12 What to take spotting
14 Looking at flowers
21 Looking at trees
32 Looking at birds
36 Looking at insects

Wild flowers

42 Yellow flowers
50 Blue flowers
54 Pink flowers
62 Purple flowers
66 Red flowers
68 White and green flowers
81 Freshwater flowers
84 Underwater plants
86 Seashore flowers

Trees

92 Conifers
110 Broadleaved trees

Birds

138 Geese, swans
140 Ducks
143 Grebes, heron, stork
144 Rails, crake
145 Cormorant, gannet, shag, chough
146 Waders
152 Gulls
153 Gull, terns
154 Auks, fulmar
155 Birds of prey
158 Owls
160 Game birds
162 Hoopoe, nightjar, cuckoo, kingfisher

163 Woodpeckers
164 Swift, swallow, martins
165 Larks, pipits, dunnock
166 Wagtails
167 Waxwing, dipper, wren, shrikes
168 Warblers
170 Flycatchers, chats
172 Thrushes, oriole
173 Thrushes, starling
174 Tits
175 Tit, nuthatch, crests, treecreeper
176 Finches
178 Crossbill, crows
180 Pigeons, doves
181 Sparrows, buntings

Bugs & insects

184 Butterflies
190 Moths

200 Beetles
209 Bugs
214 Dragonflies and damselflies
216 Bees, wasps, ants
220 Ant, sawfly, gallwasps
221 True flies
224 Ant-lion, lacewings
225 Scorpion fly, alder fly, snake fly
226 Caddis fly, stonefly, mayfly
227 Crickets
228 Grasshopper, bush crickets
229 Cockroaches, mantis
230 Stick insect, earwigs
231 Some other small insects

232 Scorecard
244 Useful words
250 Index

How to use this book

There are thousands of plants and animals in the British Isles and other parts of Europe. This book will help you identify some of the most common and a few of the rarer ones, too.

The guide is divided into four sections: flowers, trees, birds and insects.

Identification

Each different kind of plant or animal is called a species. All the species in this book have a picture and a description to help you to identify them. The example below shows you how the descriptions work.

Keeping a record

Next to each picture and description is a small blank circle. Whenever you spot a new species, you can put a tick in the circle to remind you of what you have seen.

Useful words

On pages 244-249 there is a list of words that you may not have met before. Look here if you read something you don't understand.

Picture of species (not drawn to scale)

Name and description
of species

➤ Scarlet pimpernel

Grows along the ground. Flowers close in bad weather. Black dots under the pointed, oval leaves. Cultivated land. ——— Where to
15cm tall. June-Aug.   find species

Flowers may
also be blue

Close-up of species with
additional information
to help identify it

Average   When to see   Circle to tick when
size   plant in flower you spot this species

➡ Flower descriptions

Most of the flowers that grow inland are arranged by colour, to make it easy for you to look them up. There are also separate pages where you can find out about some common plants that grow in water or by the seashore.

The last line of the descriptions tells you the months you usually see each plant in flower. The rest of the plant can often be seen at other times of the year.

Primrose

To find out more about identifying flowers, turn to pages 14-20.

You can find out more about spotting trees on pages 21-31.

English oak

⬅ Tree descriptions

Next to each tree picture, you can see its bark, leaves and fruits and sometimes its flowers as well. A small picture next to some trees shows how they look when they lose all their leaves in winter.

➡ Bird descriptions

You'll find similar birds
grouped together, so
for example, all the
finches can be found
on the same pages.
Some descriptions
have extra pictures
to help you tell
very similar
species apart.

Bewick's
swan
122cm

Whooper
swan
152cm

Mute
swan
152cm

There is more
information about
looking at birds on
pages 32-35.

⬅ Insect descriptions

Small white

With some birds and insects,
the male ♂ and female ♀
look different. In this case,
both sexes are illustrated
and identified by their
symbols. Most of the insects
are shown much bigger
then they really are. Look
at the measurement
to check their
real size.

♂

♀

♂

♀

Turn to pages
36-39 to
find out more
about insects.

What lives where

The species in this book can all be found in Europe. Not all the species that live in each country are in the book, and some are not found everywhere in Europe.

Some species are more common in one country than another. A few animals and plants will be very rare in the British Isles, but you can keep an eye out for them when you visit other European countries.

Scandinavia

British Isles

Mainland Europe

The green area on this map shows the countries covered by this book.

Scorecard

At the end of this book there is a scorecard, which gives you an idea of how common each species is. A common type scores 5 points, and a rare one is worth 25 points. If you like, you can add up your score after a day out spotting.

Some species may not be common where you live. Try to spot them if you go on holiday. Other species are rare in the wild.

Species (name)	Score	Date spotted
Barberry	15	20/05
Barnacle goose	15	26/01
Barn owl	20	
Bar-tailed godwit	15	
Bats-in-the-belfry	15	17/08
Bean aphid	5	

You can fill in the scorecard like this.

You could count rare species if you see them in a garden or on television.

When and where to spot

When to go spotting

The best time to go spotting is in spring and summer when plants are flowering and many animals are breeding.

Winter is also a good time for spotting birds, especially early in the morning and at dusk. It is also surprisingly easy to identify trees in winter, by looking at their leafless outlines and the way their branches are arranged.

A place to live

Birds, trees, flowers and insects are almost everywhere, which makes spotting them a good hobby, no matter where you live. The places where plants and animals live are known as habitats. If you go away from home, you will be able to see new species when you visit new habitats.

Towns and cities

If you live in a town or a city there are plenty of places to go spotting. Try looking in parks, gardens, churchyards, playing fields, or see what you can find in waste places, and along canals and rivers.

In the country

The countryside contains a huge variety of habitats. Fields, hedgerows and woodland are particularly rich in things to spot. There are plenty of things to find in bleaker and wilder places such as moors, mountains, marshes and seashores, too. Lakes, ponds and streams are also home to a wide range of plants and animals.

Do not disturb

When you go out spotting be as quiet as possible. It is important not to frighten or disturb any of the wildlife you find. For example, it is illegal to disturb breeding birds, their nests or their eggs.

Make sure you don't touch any of the animals you are trying to identify, or pick any wild flowers. It's better to leave them growing where everyone can enjoy them.

Spotting safely

• Always take a friend or an adult out spotting with you and make sure you tell someone else where you are going.
• Wear comfortable clothes and shoes, suitable for outdoors.
• Never go into water, even if it looks shallow.
• Don't use logs or stones as stepping-stones as they may move.

What to take spotting

It's useful to take the following things with you when you're out spotting:

- this book
- a notepad and a pencil, so that you can record your finds
- a tape measure or clear plastic ruler, to measure the things you find
- a magnifying glass, so you can examine individual flowers and insects
- a camera to take photos of things you see
- binoculars, if you have them, for birdwatching

Keeping records

It can be useful to keep notes of the things you spot, and you might even decide to make a nature diary. You could draw a picture of the species you have seen, and note down when and where you found it. Jot down how long or tall it is, as well as its colour, markings and anything else that takes your interest.

You can stick photos, maps, feathers and leaves into your nature diary

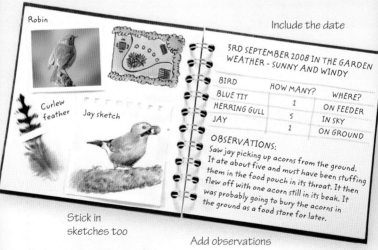

Robin

Curlew feather

Jay sketch

Include the date

3RD SEPTEMBER 2008 IN THE GARDEN
WEATHER - SUNNY AND WINDY

BIRD	HOW MANY?	WHERE?
BLUE TIT	1	ON FEEDER
HERRING GULL	5	IN SKY
JAY	1	ON GROUND

OBSERVATIONS:
Saw jay picking up acorns from the ground. It ate about five and must have been stuffing them in the food pouch in its throat. It then flew off with one acorn still in its beak. It was probably going to bury the acorns in the ground as a food store for later.

Stick in sketches too

Add observations

12

Measuring plants and animals

The plants and animals in this book are not drawn to scale, but the average size of each species is given in the description beside it. The measurements are given in millimetres (mm), centimetres (cm) or metres (m) and the pictures below show you how they are measured.

Birds and insects – total body length (including tail but not legs)

Butterflies, moths and dragonflies – distance across wingspan (W.S.)

Plants and trees – height from ground or water-level or width of flowerhead

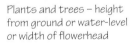

Looking at flowers

These pictures show some different kinds of flowers, and explain some of the words that appear in the book. When you are examining a plant, look closely at the flowerhead to help you to identify it.

Some flowers have petals of even length and lots of stamens.

Buttercup

Petal —

All the petals together are called the corolla

— Stamens

— Bud

The petals of some flowers are joined together.

Foxglove

— Bract

— Sepal

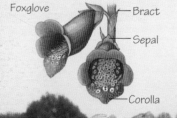

— Corolla

Some flowerheads are made up of clusters of tiny flowers.

Daisy

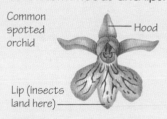

Centre is really lots of tiny flowers

Some flowers have petals which form hoods and lips.

Common spotted orchid

— Hood

Lip (insects land here) —

Toadflax

The petals of some flowers form a tube called a spur.

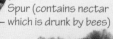

Spur (contains nectar which is drunk by bees)

Shapes to look for

These pictures show some of the different ways that plants grow. Looking out for these shapes will help you to recognize different plants.

An "erect" plant grows straight up from the ground. "Runners" are stems that grow sideways along the ground, as though they are creeping. Some plants grow in thick mats or carpets close to the ground. These are called "mat-forming" plants.

An erect plant

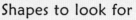

Early purple orchid

A plant with runners

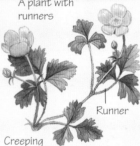

Runner

A mat-forming plant

Creeping buttercup

Stonecrop

Inside a flower

This is what the inside of a buttercup looks like. The stigma, style and ovary form the female part of the flower, or "carpel".

The stamens are the male parts. Pollen from the stamens is received by the stigma (this is called pollination). It causes seeds to grow inside the ovary.

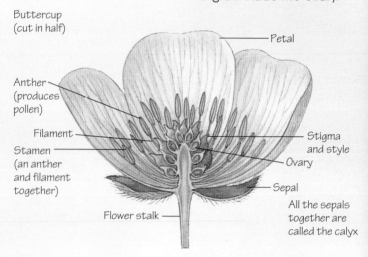

Buttercup
(cut in half)

Petal

Anther
(produces
pollen)

Filament

Stamen
(an anther
and filament
together)

Stigma
and style

Ovary

Sepal

Flower stalk

All the sepals together are called the calyx

Some flowers can pollinate themselves and some are pollinated by wind. Other flowers need insects to spread their pollen. These flowers have special scents and markings to attract insects.

The scent and colour of this meadow clary flower have attracted a bee

Pollen brushes onto the bee; when it visits another flower, the stigma will pick up this pollen from its body

From flower to fruit

A flower helps a plant to produce seeds. Once a flower is pollinated, the seeds start to develop and the petals wither and fall off. The rest of the flower becomes a fruit containing seeds.

A bee pollinates the poppy flower

The petals and stamens die

The ovary swells and develops into a fruit

Fruits and seeds

The seeds of a plant are usually surrounded by a fruit. Different plants have different-looking fruits, so you can recognize plants by their fruits. Here are two examples.

Blackberry fruit (the seeds are inside)

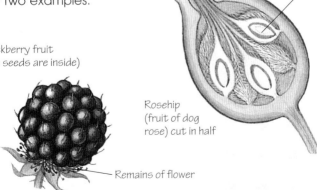

Remains of flower

Seed

Rosehip (fruit of dog rose) cut in half

Remains of flower

Leaves

Even if a plant is not in flower, you can recognize it from its leaves. There are many different leaf shapes.

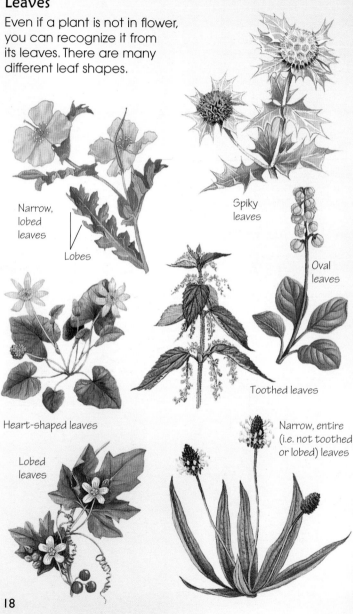

Narrow, lobed leaves

Lobes

Spiky leaves

Oval leaves

Toothed leaves

Heart-shaped leaves

Lobed leaves

Narrow, entire (i.e. not toothed or lobed) leaves

Leaves can also be arranged in different ways on the stem of a plant.

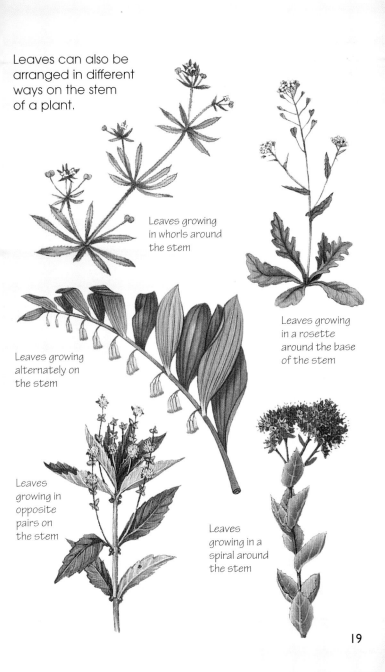

Leaves growing in whorls around the stem

Leaves growing alternately on the stem

Leaves growing in a rosette around the base of the stem

Leaves growing in opposite pairs on the stem

Leaves growing in a spiral around the stem

19

Protecting wild flowers

Be careful not to tread on young plants or to break their stems.

Many wild plants that were once common are now rare, because people have picked and dug up so many. It is now against the law to dig up any wild plant by the roots, or to pick certain rare plants such as red helleborine. If you pick wild flowers, they will die. Leave them for others to enjoy. It is much better to draw or photograph flowers, so that you and other people can see them again.

These flowers are all rare in the wild.

Corky-fruited water dropwort

Pasque flower

Cornflower

If you think you have found a rare plant, let your local nature conservation club know about it as soon as you can, so they can help protect it. You can get their address from your local library or look on the internet. There are links to some useful websites on the Usborne Quicklinks website at www.usborne-quicklinks.com.

Looking at trees

This book will help you identify some of the trees of Britain and Europe. Not all the trees will be common in your area, but you may be able to find many of them in large gardens and parks.

What to look for

There are lots of clues to help you identify a tree – whatever the time of year.

Yew

Oak

Common beech

In spring and summer, look at the leaves and flowers. In autumn, look out for fruits, and in winter examine twigs, buds, bark and tree shape.

Conifer or broadleaf?

The trees in this book are divided into two main groups: conifers and broadleaves.

Conifers have narrow, needle-like or scaly leaves, and their fruits are usuallly woody cones. Most conifers are evergreen, which means they keep their leaves in winter. Their shape is more regular than broadleaved trees.

Sitka spruce

Broadleaved trees have broad, flat leaves and seeds enclosed in fruits, such as nuts. Most are deciduous, which means they lose their leaves in autumn.

Sweet chestnut

Leaves

Leaves will often give you the biggest clue to the identity of a tree. Be careful, though, because some trees have very similar leaves. There are many different types of leaves. Here are some of the most common ones.

Simple leaves

A leaf that is in one piece is called a simple leaf. Simple leaves can be many shapes: round, oval, triangular, heart-shaped, or long and narrow. The edges are sometimes spiky (like holly) or toothed (slightly jagged). Some leaves have very wavy edges, called lobes.

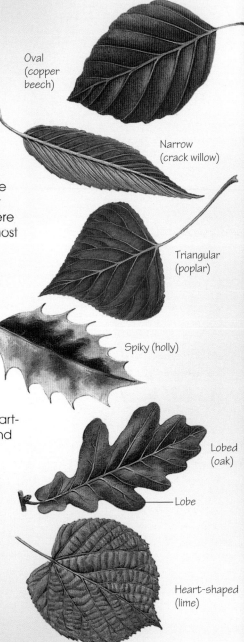

Oval (copper beech)

Narrow (crack willow)

Triangular (poplar)

Spiky (holly)

Lobed (oak)

Lobe

Heart-shaped (lime)

Compound leaves

A leaf that is made up of smaller leaves, or leaflets, is called a compound leaf.

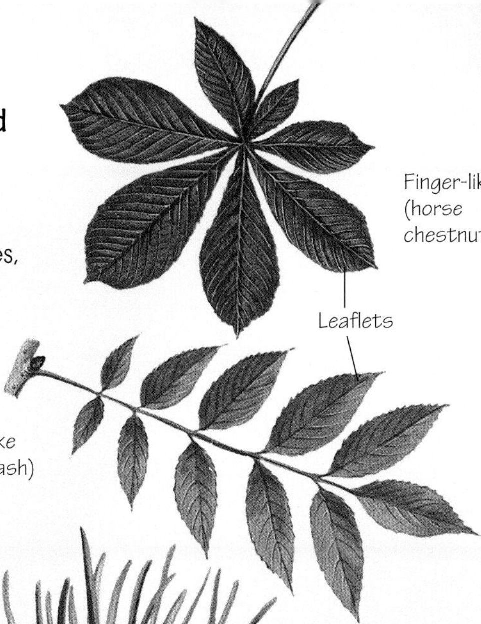

Finger-like (horse chestnut)

Leaflets

Feather-like (common ash)

Conifer leaves

Many conifers have narrow, needle-like leaves – either single, in small bunches, or in clusters. They can be very sharp and spiky. Some conifers, such as cypresses, have tiny scale-like leaves, which overlap one another.

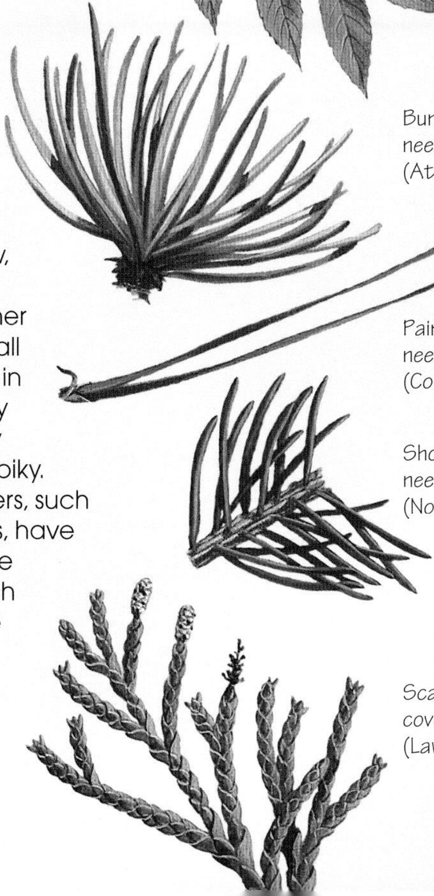

Bunch of needles (Atlas cedar)

Pair of long needles (Corsican pine)

Short single needles (Norway spruce)

Scale-like leaves covering twigs (Lawson cypress)

23

Flowers

All trees produce flowers that later develop into fruits, though some flowers are so small you can hardly see them. Most flowers have both male and female parts. A few species, such as holly, have male and female flowers on separate trees.

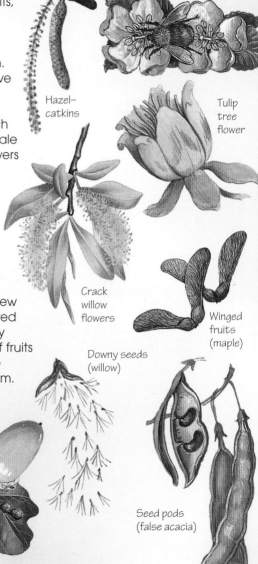

Crab apple blossom

Hazel-catkins

Tulip tree flower

Crack willow flowers

Fruits and seeds

Fruits contain the seeds that can grow into new trees. Broadleaved trees have many different kinds of fruits and seeds. Here are some of them.

Winged fruits (maple)

Downy seeds (willow)

Acorn (oak)

Seed pods (false acacia)

Crab apple

Soft fruit (cherry)

Soft fruit (pear)

Conker (horse chestnut)

"Bobble" fruit (plane)

Berries (holly)

Cones in bunches (Norway spruce)

Cones

Conifers produce woody fruits called cones, made up of many overlapping scales containing seeds. At the base of each scale is a leaf-like part called a bract. Cones come in different shapes and sizes, and only some have visible bracts.

Seed

Bract

Scale

Cone (Douglas fir)

Scots pine cone seeds falling out

Finding the right tree

The trees in this book are divided into conifers and broadleaves, with more closely related trees, such as all the oaks, grouped together. If you spot a tree you can't identify, but you know what type of leaf it has, you can use this chart to help you match it up with a tree in this book. The numbers show where you'll find the illustration.

Broadleaves

Simple

Unlobed leaves

Common alder	114	Silver birch	118
Common beech	121	Common pear	122
Southern beech	120	Holly	132
Crab apple	122	Aspen	116
Holm oak	111	Western balsam poplar	117
Whitebeam	115	Goat willow	119
Black Italian poplar	116	White willow	120
Lombardy poplar	118	Silver lime	126
Crack willow	119	Wych elm	127
Common lime	126	Wild cherry	129
English elm	127	Black mulberry	130
Sweet chestnut	128	Cork oak	112
Bird cherry	129	Blackthorn	123
Grey alder	114	Magnolia	135
Hornbeam	121		

Lobed leaves

English oak	110	Sessile oak	110
Red oak	112	Turkey oak	111
White poplar	117	London plane	124
Sycamore	124	Norway maple	125
Field maple	125	Tulip tree	134
Maidenhair tree	134	Hawthorn	123

Compound

Leaves with a central stem

Common ash	113
Rowan	115
False acacia	131
Manna ash	113
Common walnut	130
Tree of Heaven	135

Finger-like

Horse chestnut	128
Laburnum	131

Conifers

Single needles

Norway spruce 96	Grand fir 100
European silver fir 98	Douglas fir 101
Noble fir 100	Juniper 105
Western hemlock 101	Coast redwood 107
Yew 106	Greek fir 99
Sitka spruce 96	Spanish fir 99

Needles grouped in 2s

Scots pine 92
Maritime pine 92
Stone pine 93
Shore pine 93
Corsican pine 94
Aleppo pine 94

Needles grouped in 3s

Monterey pine 95

Needles grouped in 5s

Swiss stone pine..95

Needles in more than 5s - Evergreen

Atlas cedar 108
Cedar of Lebanon 108
Deodar cedar 109

Needles in more than 5s - Deciduous

European larch 97
Japanese larch 97

Other conifers

Swamp cypress 104
Dawn redwood 106

Scale-like leaves

Nootka cypress 98	Western red cedar 102
Lawson cypress 102	Italian cypress 103
Monterey cypress 103	Leyland cypress 104
Japanese red cedar 105	Wellingtonia 107
Chile pine 109	

What else to look for?

Although the most obvious way to identify a tree is by its leaves, there are lots of other features to look out for too.

Tree shape

You can sometimes tell a tree by its shape, especially in winter when many trees are bare. The leafy top of a tree is called its crown, and each type of tree has its own particular crown shape. This comes from the arrangement of its branches.

Twigs

Look closely at the way the leaves are arranged on the twigs. On some trees, they grow opposite each other in matching pairs. On other trees, the leaves are single and alternate from one side of the twig to the other.

The leaves of a silver birch alternate from one side of the twig to the other.

Cone-shaped
(Norway spruce)

Narrow crown
(Lombardy poplar)

The leaves of a horse chestnut grow opposite each other in pairs.

Broad crown
(Oak)

Bark

The outside of a tree is covered in a hard, tough layer of bark, which protects the tree from drying out and from damage by insects and other animals. The type of bark a tree has can give clues to its identity too.

Silver birch peels off in wispy strips that look like ribbons.

The bark of Scots pine flakes off in large pieces.

English oak has deep ridges and cracks.

Beech has smooth thin bark, which flakes off in tiny pieces.

On the right is a cross-section of a tree trunk, showing the different layers, or rings. Each year, the trunk thickens by growing a new layer.

Identifying winter buds

Most broadleaved trees have no leaves in winter, but you can often identify them by their winter buds. These contain the beginnings of next year's shoot, leaves and flowers.

What shape is the twig? What colour are the buds, and are they pointed or rounded? Are they positioned in opposite pairs, or single and alternate? Is the bud covered with hairs or scales? If scales, how many are there? Is the bud sticky?

False acacia

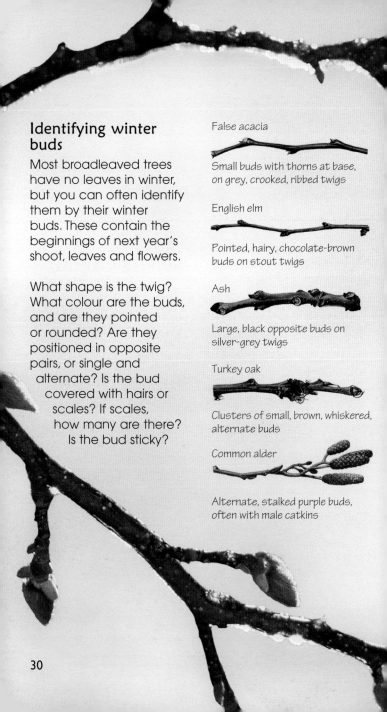

Small buds with thorns at base, on grey, crooked, ribbed twigs

English elm

Pointed, hairy, chocolate-brown buds on stout twigs

Ash

Large, black opposite buds on silver-grey twigs

Turkey oak

Clusters of small, brown, whiskered, alternate buds

Common alder

Alternate, stalked purple buds, often with male catkins

White poplar

Small, orange-brown buds covered by white, felty hairs on green twigs

Sweet chestnut

Rounded, reddish-brown buds on knobbly, greenish-brown twigs

Common beech

Long, pointed, copper-brown buds sticking out from brown twigs

London plane

Alternate, brown cone-shaped buds with ring scars around them

Sycamore

Large green, opposite buds, with dark-edged scales on stout, light-brown twigs

Common walnut

Big, black, velvety triangle-shaped, alternate buds on thick, hollow twigs

Whitebeam

Downy, green, alternate buds

White willow

Slender buds enclosed in a single scale, close to pinkish, downy twigs

Common lime

Zigzag twig. Alternate, reddish buds with two scales

Wild cherry

Fat, shiny, red-brown buds grouped at the tips of light brown twigs

31

Looking at birds

When you are trying to identify a bird, ask yourself these questions: What size and shape is it? What colour is it? Does it have any special markings? Where does it live? How does it feed? How does it fly?

Remember that in some cases the males and females of a species look different from each other. In this book these symbols are used show which is which:

♂ = Male

♀ = Female

Be aware that some species have different plumages (feathers) in summer and winter.

Ruff in summer

Ruff in winter

♀

Female chaffinch

Male chaffinch

♂

Juvenile ringed plover

Adult ringed plover

Also remember that the young birds (juveniles) of some species look different from the adults.

The parts of a bird

Although birds vary from species to species, they all have wings, feathers and a beak. To describe birds accurately, it's useful to know the names of some of their other parts too.

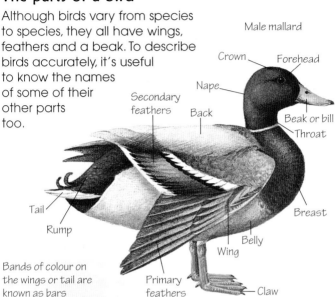

Male mallard

Crown

Forehead

Nape

Secondary feathers

Back

Beak or bill

Throat

Breast

Belly

Wing

Tail

Rump

Bands of colour on the wings or tail are known as bars

Primary feathers

Claw

Binoculars

As you do more birdwatching, you will probably want to use binoculars. Visit a good shop and try out several pairs. The best sizes are 8x30 or 8x40 (never more than 10x50 or they will be too heavy).

Make sure your binoculars are light enough to carry around with you.

Migration

Migration is the making of regular journeys from one place to another and back again. Some birds migrate in spring and autumn. In Europe birds usually travel between a summer breeding area and a wintering area in Africa.

Why migrate?

Birds migrate in autumn when food, such as insects, becomes hard to find. It is food shortages rather than cold weather which cause migration.

Finding their way

Scientists don't fully understand how birds can navigate over such huge distances, but they have come up with a few theories. Some species might use a combination of these methods.

Some birds that migrate during the day might follow landmarks, such as mountains and islands. The position of the Moon and stars may help night-fliers to find their way. Research on pigeons suggests that they are guided by lines of magnetic forces from the centre of the Earth.

Returning home

The birds return in spring when food supplies have built up again. By doing so, the birds feed better and face less competition for food from other animals. If they travel northwards, they have more daylight in which to hunt and feed their young.

Irruptions

Irruptions are irregular journeys from the usual range. They are usually caused by changes in the food supply. Snowy owls, for instance, irrupt well to the south of their normal wintering range when their usual food sources are scarce.

Recording birds

Much of the information about migration comes from ringing schemes in which birds are caught and carefully fitted with metal leg rings by trained ringers. Each ring bears a unique number and address.

Finding and reporting ringed birds tells us a great deal about the age and movement of the birds. Wing tags bearing numbers or letters can be read with binoculars so that the birds don't need to be caught. Tracking individual birds on their flight paths is also possible if a small radio transmitter is attached to each bird.

Whooper swans setting out on their long flight from Iceland to the UK, where they will spend the winter

Looking at insects

All adult insects have six legs and their bodies have three distinct parts – a head, a thorax and an abdomen.

As you will see in this book, though, different kinds of insect look very different from each other. Bugs are just one kind of insect.

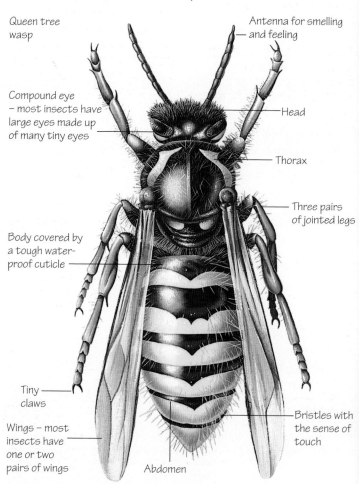

Queen tree wasp

Antenna for smelling and feeling

Compound eye – most insects have large eyes made up of many tiny eyes

Head

Thorax

Three pairs of jointed legs

Body covered by a tough water-proof cuticle

Tiny claws

Wings – most insects have one or two pairs of wings

Abdomen

Bristles with the sense of touch

An insect's life-cycle

Most insects hatch from eggs. After hatching, they go through different stages of growth before becoming adults.

The eggs of some insects, such as butterflies and beetles, pass through two more stages before becoming adults – a larva stage and a pupa stage.

Some insects, such as bugs and dragonflies, lay eggs that hatch into larvae called nymphs. Nymphs look like small adults. They shed their skin several times, each time growing bigger. This is called moulting. A nymph's wings start as tiny buds, which grow bigger each time it moults.

These three pictures show a larva developing into a swallowtail butterfly

This grasshopper nymph looks very like an adult grasshopper, but it does not have wings

1. The egg hatches into a larva known as a caterpillar

2. The caterpillar becomes a pupa. Inside the pupa, the body of the caterpillar breaks down and becomes the body of the butterfly

3. The pupa splits and an adult emerges

Food and feeding

Insects feed on all kinds of animals and plants. Insects are carnivores (meat-eaters), herbivores (plant-eaters) or omnivores (meat- and plant-eaters). Some insects, known as parasites, actually live on or inside the bodies of other living animals.

Insect mouthparts

Insects use their mouthparts to suck up liquids, or to bite and chew solid food. Insects that suck have a hollow tube called a proboscis. Bees, butterflies and moths use a proboscis to suck nectar from flowers.

Bee

Proboscis

Butterflies have a coiled proboscis

House-flies have suction pads at the end of their proboscises. Saliva passes into the pad and partly digests food before it is sucked into the fly's mouth.

House-fly

Sucking pad

Some insects pierce plants and animals with a pointed tube called a rostrum.

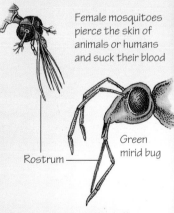

Female mosquitoes pierce the skin of animals or humans and suck their blood

Rostrum

Green mirid bug

Insects, such as beetles, that bite and chew have strong jaws.

Beetle's jaws

Self-defence

All insects are in constant danger of being eaten by other animals. Here are some of the ways they defend themselves.

Shock tactics

Some insects sting, bite, or produce nasty smells or poisons to shock their enemies and give them time to escape. Others try to look dangerous, or make sudden movements to frighten their enemies.

A bombardier beetle fires a puff of poisonous gas at its enemies

Colour warning

Insects that taste unpleasant are often brightly coloured so that predators will avoid eating them. Some harmless insects protect themselves by copying the colours of bad-tasting or poisonous insects.

Camouflage

The colour of many insects makes them difficult for predators to spot.

The poplar hawk moth caterpillar is well-disguised by colours and markings which match the leaves it feeds on

Shape can also be a camouflage. For example, stick insects and some caterpillars resemble twigs. Other insects can look like leaves, grass or seeds.

Stick insects look so like twigs they are hard to detect

Wild
Flowers

Yellow flowers

Look for these flowers in damp places, such as ditches, marshes and water meadows.

➡ Lesser celandine

A small, creeping plant with glossy, heart-shaped leaves. Shiny yellow flowers. Look in damp, shady woods and waysides. 7cm tall. March-May.

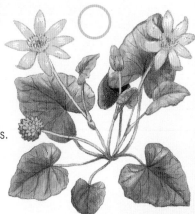

Each flower has four yellow sepals

⬅ Alternate-leaved golden saxifrage

Small plant with round, toothed leaves and greenish-yellow flowers. Look in wet places. 7cm tall. April-July.

➡ Creeping buttercup

Look for the long runners near the ground. Hairy, deeply divided leaves. Shiny yellow flowers. Common weed of grassy places. May-Aug.

Runner

➡ Creeping Jenny

A creeping, mat-forming plant with shiny, oval leaves. Yellow flowers are 1.5-2.5cm across. In grassy places and under hedges. June-Aug.

Opposite leaves

➡ Cowslip

Easily recognized in April and May by the single clusters of nodding flowers. Rosette of leaves at base. Grows in meadows. 15cm tall.

Sepals

Close-up of flower

⬅ Common meadow rue

Tall, erect plant with dense clusters of flowers. Leaves have 3-4 lobes. Look in marshy fields and fens. Up to 80cm tall. July-Aug.

43

Yellow flowers

Look for these flowers in woods, hedgerows and heaths.

Cluster of fruits

➡ Herb Bennet or wood avens

Fruits have hooks which catch on clothes and animals' fur. Woods, hedges and shady places. Up to 50cm tall. June-Aug.

⬅ Yellow pimpernel

Like creeping Jenny, but smaller, with more pointed leaves. Slender, trailing stems. The flowers close in dull weather. Woods and hedges. May-Sept.

Barberries can be used to make jam

➡ Barberry

A shrub with spiny branches. Bees visit the drooping flowers. Look for the red berries. Hedges and scrubland. Up to 100cm tall. May-June.

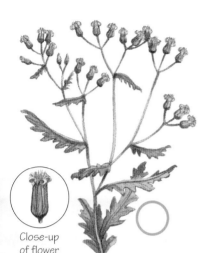

Close-up
of flower

← Wood groundsel

Erect plant growing
on heaths and sandy
soil. The petals of the
small flowers curl back.
Narrow lobed leaves.
60cm tall. July-Sept.

Whorl of
flowers

→ Yellow archangel

Also called weasel-snout.
Look for the red-brown
markings on the yellow
petals. Opposite pairs of
leaves. Common in woods.
40cm tall. May-June.

← Primrose

Well-known spring flower,
with hairy stems and
rosette of large leaves.
Often grows in patches.
Woods, hedges and
fields. 15cm tall.
Dec-May.

Yellow flowers

Look for these flowers in open, grassy places, such as heaths and commons.

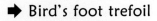

◣ Furze

Also called gorse or whin. Dark green, spiny bush on heaths and commons. The bright yellow flowers smell like coconut. 100-200cm tall. March-June.

Close-up of flower

➧ Bird's foot trefoil

Also called bacon and eggs because the yellow flowers are streaked with red. Look for this small, creeping plant on grassy banks and downs. May-June.

The seed pods look like birds' claws

Seeds

Silverweed

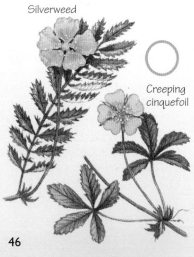

Creeping cinquefoil

◄ Creeping cinquefoil

Like silverweed, spreads close to the ground with long, rooting runners. Hedge banks and grassy places. May-Aug.

← Common St. John's wort

Look for see-through dots on the narrow, oval leaves, and black dots on the petals and sepals. Damp, grassy places. 60cm tall. June-Sept.

→ Woad

Look for the hanging pods on this tall, erect plant. The leaves were once boiled to make a blue dye. Waysides and dry places. 70cm tall. June-Sept.

Seed pod

Dandelion "clock"

← Dandelion

Common weed with rosette of toothed leaves. The flowers close at night. Look for the "clock" of downy white fruits. Waysides. 15cm tall. March-June.

Close-up of fruit

Yellow flowers

➡ Stonecrop

Also called wallpepper.
Mat-forming plant with
star-shaped flowers.
The thick, fleshy leaves
have a peppery taste.
Dunes, shingle and
walls. June-July.

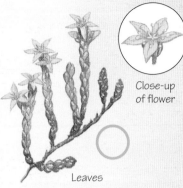

Close-up
of flower

Leaves

⬅ Purslane

A low, spreading plant
with red stems. The fleshy,
oval-shaped leaves are
in opposite pairs. A weed
of fields and waste places.
May-Oct.

Close-up
of flower

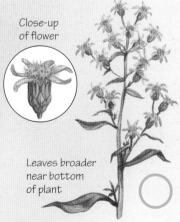

➡ Golden rod

Erect plant with flowers
on thin spikes. Leaves
are narrower and more
pointed near top of plant.
Woods, banks and cliffs.
40cm tall. July-Sept.

Leaves broader
near bottom
of plant

Close-up of seed pod

◀ Rape

Common on roadsides, fields and motorways. Also grown as a crop. Dark blue-green leaves. Flowers grow in clusters and have four petals. Look for the long seed pods. Up to 100cm tall. May-July.

➡ Cypress spurge

Erect plant with many pale, needle-like leaves. Spray of yellowish flowers. Roadsides and grassy places. Rare in Britain. 40cm tall. May-Aug.

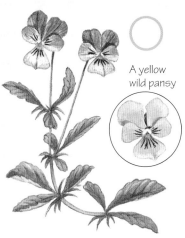

A yellow wild pansy

◀ Wild pansy or heartsease

The flowers can be violet, yellow, or a mixture of both, or sometimes pink and white. Grassy places and cornfields. 15cm tall. April-Oct.

Blue flowers

← Cornflower

Also called bluebottle.
Erect plant with greyish,
downy leaves and a
blue flower head.
Cornfields and waste
places. 40cm tall.
July-Aug. Rare.

Spur

➤ Larkspur

Slender plant with
divided, feathery leaves.
The flowers have a long
spur. Cultivated land.
50cm tall. June-July.

Seed
pod

Bud

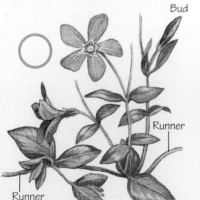

← Lesser periwinkle

Creeps along the ground
with long runners, making
leafy carpets. Shiny,
oval leaves. Woods and
hedges. Flower stems up
to 15cm tall. Feb-May.

Runner

Runner

➡ Viper's bugloss

Long, narrow leaves on rough, hairy stems. Erect or creeping. Pink buds become blue flowers. Waysides and sand dunes. 30cm tall. June-Sept.

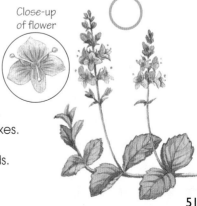

Bud

Stamens

Sharp hairs on stem

⬅ Common forget-me-not

The curled stems of this hairy plant slowly straighten when it flowers. Flowers turn from pink to blue. Open places. 20cm tall. April-Oct.

Flowers have yellow centres

Rosette of leaves

Close-up of flower

➡ Common speedwell

A hairy plant which forms large mats. Pinkish-blue flowers on erect spikes. Opposite, oval leaves. Grassy places and woods. 30cm tall. May-Aug.

51

Blue flowers

Look for these flowers in damp places.

Flower is shaped like a monk's hood

➡ Brooklime

Creeping plant with erect, reddish stems. Shiny, oval leaves in opposite pairs. Used to be eaten in salads. Wet places. 30cm tall. May-Sept.

Close-up of bugle-shaped flower

🏹 Common monkshood

Also called wolfsbane. Upright plant with spike of flowers at end of stem. Notice hood on flowers and the deeply-divided leaves. Near streams and in damp woods. 70cm tall. June-Sept.

⬅ Bugle

Creeping plant with erect flower spikes. Glossy leaves in opposite pairs. Stem is square and hairy on two sides. Leaves and stem are purplish. Forms carpets in damp woods. 20cm tall. May-June.

➡ Water forget-me-not

Grows in damp shady places next to still or running water. Blue flowers that may be pink at first. Flowers about 1cm across. June-Oct.

Flowers grow in whorls

⬅ Meadow clary or meadow sage

Hairy stem with wrinkled leaves mostly at the base of the plant. Grassy places. 40cm tall. June-July.

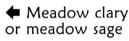

➡ Bluebell

Also called wild hyacinth. Narrow, shiny leaves and clusters of nodding blue flowers. Forms thick carpets in woods. 30cm tall. April-May.

Close-up of fruit

Pink flowers

Look for these flowers in woods or hedges.

➡ Wood sorrel

A creeping, woodland plant with slender stems and rounded leaves. The white flowers have purplish veins. Woods and hedges. 10cm tall. April-May.

⬅ Red helleborine

Upright plant with pointed leaves and a fleshy stem. Rare plant, protected by law. Woods and shady places. Up to 40cm tall. May-June.

➡ Blackberry or bramble

Dense, woody plant that climbs up hedges. Sharp prickles on stems and under leaves. Berries are ripe and good to eat in autumn. June-Sept.

Ripe berry

← Bistort

Also called snakeweed.
Forms patches. Leaves
are narrow. Flowers in
spikes. In meadows,
often near water.
40cm tall. June-Oct.

→ Greater bindweed

Look for the large, pink
or white funnel-shaped
flowers. Climbs walls and
hedges in waste places.
Leaves are shaped like
arrowheads. 300cm high.
July-Sept.

Bud

← Dog rose

Scrambling creeper,
up to 300cm tall,
with thorny stems.
Look for the red fruits,
called rose hips, in
autumn. Hedges and
woods. June-July.

Rose hip
(fruit)

55

Pink flowers

➡ Knotgrass

A weed that spreads
in a thick mat or
grows erect. Waste
ground, fields and
seashores. Stems can
be 100cm long.
July-Oct.

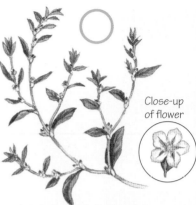

Close-up
of flower

⬅ Soapwort

Erect plant with clusters
of scented flowers. The
broad, oval leaves were
once used to make soap.
Near rivers and streams.
40cm tall. Aug-Oct.

Bud

➡ Common fumitory

Creeping plant with
much-divided, feathery
leaves. Tiny flowers are
tube-shaped and tipped
with purple. Cultivated
land. 30cm tall. May-Oct.

Close-up
of flower

➡ Sand spurrey

Spreading, mat-forming plant with sticky, hairy stems. Narrow, grey-green leaves end in a stiff point. Sandy places. 10cm tall. May-Sept.

Seed with hairy "parachute"

⬅ Rosebay willowherb

Also called fireweed. Tall, erect plant with spikes of pink flowers. Long, narrow leaves. Common on waste ground. 90cm tall. July-Sept.

Close-up of flower

Sepals

➡ Herb Robert

Spreading plant with a strong smell. The flowers droop at night and in bad weather. Leaves are red in autumn. Woods and hedgebanks. 40cm tall. May-Sept.

Pink flowers

Look for these flowers on heaths and moors.

Close-up
of flower

📍 Heather or ling

Shrubby plant with small, narrow leaves. Grows on heaths and moors. Leafy spikes of pink or white flowers. 20cm tall. July-Sept.

➡ Bell heather

Like heather, but taller. Thin, needle-like leaves and clusters of bell-shaped, pink flowers. Dry heaths and moors. 30cm tall. July-Aug.

Close-up
of flower

The berries
are edible

◀ Bilberry

Small shrub with oval leaves. Drooping, bell-shaped, green-pink flowers. Heaths, moors and woods. 40cm tall. April-June.

Look for these flowers in dry, grassy places.

➡ Sorrel

Erect plant. Arrow-shaped leaves have backward-pointing lobes. Branched spikes of flowers. Leaves are eaten in salads. Pastures. 20-100cm tall. May-July

Close-up of flower (above) and fruit (below)

Lobe

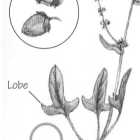

Close-up of flower (above) and fruit (below)

Lobe

⬅ Sheep's sorrel

Smaller than sorrel. The lobes on the leaves point upwards. Dry places and heaths. 30cm tall. May-Aug.

➡ Common centaury

Erect plant with rosette of leaves at base and opposite leaves on stem. Flowers close at night. Grassland, dunes and woods. 50cm tall. June-Oct.

Opposite pair of leaves

59

Pink flowers

➡ Ragged Robin

Flowers have ragged, pink petals. Erect plant with a forked stem and narrow, pointed leaves. Damp meadows, marshes and woods. 30-70cm tall. May-June.

Bract (a kind of small leaf near the flower)

Grooved stem

⬅ Knapweed or hard-head

Erect plant with brush-like, pink flowers growing from black bracts. Grassland and waysides. 40cm tall. June-Sept.

Whorl of leaves

➡ Hemp agrimony

Tough, erect plant with downy stem. Grows in patches in damp places. Attracts butterflies. Up to 120cm tall. July-Sept.

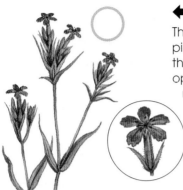

← Deptford pink

The clusters of bright pink flowers close in the afternoon. Pointed, opposite leaves. Very rare in Britain. Sandy places. 40cm tall. July-Aug.

Close-up of flower

Fruit

→ Blood-red geranium or bloody cranesbill

Bushy plant with erect or trailing stems. Deeply divided leaves are round and hairy. Hedgerows. 30cm tall. June-Aug.

Seed pod

← Red campion

Erect plant with a hairy, sticky stem and pointed, oval leaves in opposite pairs. Woodland. 60cm tall. May-June.

Purple flowers

← Early purple orchid

Erect plant with dark spots on the leaves. Smells like cats. Look for the hood and spur on the flowers. Woods and copses. Up to 60cm tall. June-Aug.

→ Tufted vetch

Scrambling plant with clinging tendrils. Climbs up hedgerows. Look for the brown seed pods in late summer. Flowers 1cm across. June-Sept.

Tendril

Policeman's helmet

Touch-me-not balsam

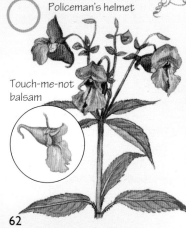

← Policeman's helmet

Also called jumping Jack. Flowers look like open mouths. Ripe seed pods explode, scattering seeds when touched. Streams. Up to 200cm tall. July-Oct.

Policeman's helmet is closely related to touch-me-not balsam

Look for these flowers in woods or hedgerows.

➡ Foxglove

Erect plant with tall spike of tube-shaped flowers, drooping on one side of the stem. Large, oval leaves. Open woods. Up to 150cm tall. June-Sept.

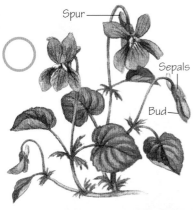

Spur

Sepals

Bud

🐾 Bats-in-the-belfry

Erect, hairy plant with large, toothed leaves. Flowers on leafy spikes point upwards. Hedges, woods and shady places. 60cm tall. July-Sept.

⬅ Common dog violet

Creeping plant with rosettes of heart-shaped leaves. Look for the pointed sepals and short spur on the flower. Woods. 10cm tall. April-June.

63

Purple flowers

Look in fields and other grassy places for these flowers.

➡ Pasque flower

Very rare in the wild, but grows in gardens. Hairy, feathery leaves. Purple or white flowers have yellow anthers. Dry, grassy places. 10cm tall. April-May.

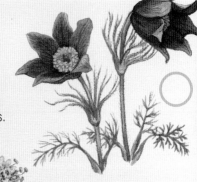

Devil's bit scabious

Field scabious

Field scabious is a similar species

⬅ Devil's bit scabious

Erect plant with narrow, pointed leaves. Flowers are pale to dark purple. Round flower heads. Wet, grassy places. 15-30cm tall. June-Oct.

Lobed leaves

Entire leaves

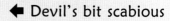

➡ Fritillary or snake's head

Drooping flowers are chequered with light and dark purple. Varies from white to dark purple. Damp meadows. 10cm tall. May.

You may see these flowers on old walls.

➡ Ivy-leaved toadflax

Weak, slender stalks trail on old walls. Look for the yellow lips on the mauve flowers. Flowers 1cm across. Shiny, ivy-shaped leaves. May-Sept.

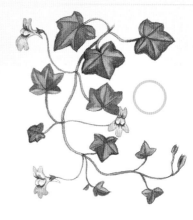

The stalk, with flowers, does not appear very often – usually you will see only the rosette

⬅ Houseleek

A rosette plant with thick, fleshy leaves. Dull red, spiky petals. Does not flower every year. Old walls and roofs. 30-60cm tall. June-July.

Rosette of leaves

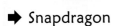

➡ Snapdragon

Erect plant with spike of flowers. Long, narrow leaves. Pouch-like flowers are yellow inside. Old walls, rocks and gardens. 40cm tall. June-Sept.

Fruit

Red flowers

Look for these flowers on cultivated land.

Flowers may also be blue

➡ Scarlet pimpernel

Grows along the ground. Flowers close in bad weather. Black dots under the pointed, oval leaves. Cultivated land. 15cm tall. June-Aug.

➡ Poppy

Erect plant with stiff hairs on stem. Soft, red flowers have dark centres. Round seed pod. Cornfields and waste ground. Up to 60cm tall. June-Aug.

Seed pod

Bud

Seed pod

⬅ Long-headed poppy

Like poppy, but flowers are paler and do not have dark centres. Pod is long and narrow. Cornfields and waste ground. Up to 45cm tall. June-Aug.

← Pheasant's eye

Rare cornfield weed with finely divided, feathery leaves. The red flowers have black centres. 20cm tall. May-Sept.

Summer pheasant's eye (not in Britain) is a similar species

➡ Sweet William

Tough, narrow leaves and flat flower cluster. Mountain pastures and cultivated land in Europe. Gardens only in Britain. 60cm tall. May-June.

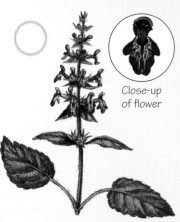

Close-up of flower

← Wood woundwort

The leaves were once used to dress wounds. Spikes of dark red and white flowers in whorls. Smells strongly. Woods. 40cm tall. June-Aug.

White and green flowers

These flowers can be found in woodlands quite early in the year.

Split petals

➡ Greater stitchwort

Look in woods and hedgerows for this slender, creeping plant. Grass-like leaves in opposite pairs. 15-60cm tall. April-June.

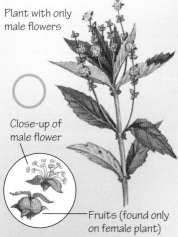
Plant with only male flowers

Close-up of male flower

Fruits (found only on female plant)

⬅ Dog's mercury

Downy plant with opposite, toothed leaves. Strong-smelling. Male flowers grow on separate plants from female flowers. Found in patches in woodlands. 15-20cm tall. Feb-April.

➡ Lily-of-the-valley

Grows in dry woods. Broad, dark green leaves and sweet-smelling flowers. Red berries in summer. Also a garden plant. 20cm tall. May-June.

Berry

➡ Ramsons or wood garlic

Smells of garlic. Broad, bright green leaves grow from a bulb. Forms carpets in damp woods, often with bluebells. 10-25cm tall. April-June.

Notice the long veins that run from one end of the leaf to the other

The large sepals look like petals

⬅ Wood anemone

Also called Granny's nightcap. Forms carpets in woods. The flowers have pink-streaked sepals. 15cm tall. March-June.

➡ Snowdrop

Welcomed as the first flower of the new year. Dark green, narrow leaves. Nodding white flowers. Woods. 20cm tall. Jan-March.

69

White and green flowers

Look for these flowers in hedges or woods.

Jack-by-the-hedge or garlic mustard

Erect plant with heart-shaped, toothed leaves. Smells of garlic. Common in hedges. Up to 120cm tall. April-June.

—Seed pod

Wild strawberry

Small plant with long, arching runners and oval, toothed leaves in threes. Sweet, red fruits, covered with seeds. Woods and scrubland. April-July.

Fruits are smaller than garden strawberries

—Tendril

Wild pea

Very rare, scrambling plant with grey-green leaves. The seeds, or peas, are inside the pods. Climbs on thickets and hedges. Up to 250cm high. June-Aug.

Pod

Look for these flowers in hedges and waysides.

➡ White bryony

Climbs up hedges with spiral tendrils. The red berries appear in August and are poisonous. Large underground stems, called tubers. Up to 400cm tall. June.

Close-up of female flower

Tendril

Berries

⬅ Cow parsley

Also called Lady's lace. Look for the ribbed stem, feathery leaves and white flower clusters. Hedge banks and ditches. Up to 100cm tall. May-June.

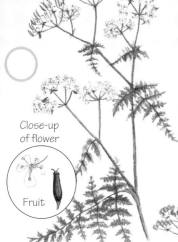

Close-up of flower

Fruit

➡ Hedge parsley

Like cow parsley, but with a stiff, hairy stem. Look for the prickly, purple fruits. Cornfields and roadsides. 60cm tall. April-May

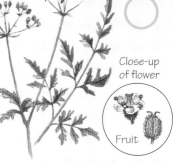

Close-up of flower

Fruit

71

White and green flowers

Look for these flowers in fields and other grassy places.

Clusters of small flowers

Close-up of single flower

Bract

Fruit

Clusters of fruits

➡ Wild carrot

Dense clusters of white flowers with a purple flower in the centre. Erect, hairy stem with feathery leaves. Grassy places, often near coast. 60cm tall. July-Aug.

Close-up of single flower

Fruit

⬅ Hogweed or keck

Very stout, hairy plant with huge leaves on long stalks. Flowers are in clusters. Grassy places and open woods. Up to 100cm tall. June-Sept.

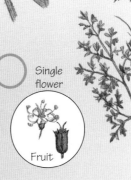

➡ Corky-fruited water dropwort

Erect plant with large, much-divided, feathery leaves. Clusters of flowers. Meadows. 60cm tall. June-Aug.

Single flower

Fruit

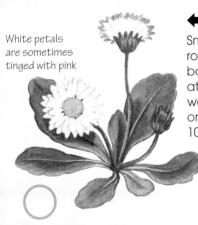

White petals are sometimes tinged with pink

← Daisy

Small plant with rosette of leaves at base. Flowers close at night and in bad weather. Very common on garden lawns. 10cm tall. Jan-Oct.

→ White or Dutch clover

Creeping plant, often grown for animal feed. Look for the white band on the three-lobed leaves. Attracts bees. 10-25cm tall. April-Aug.

White band

Runner

Look for the divided petals

← Field mouse-ear chickweed

Creeping plant with erect stems. Narrow, downy leaves. Grassy places. 10cm tall. April-Aug.

White and green flowers

Look for these flowers on cultivated land, waste land and waysides.

Close-up
of flower

➡ Pigweed or common amaranth

Erect, hairy plant with large, oval leaves. Large spikes of green, tufty flowers. Look for it on cultivated land. 50cm tall. July-Sept.

Single flower

Fruit

Cluster of flowers

🡔 Common orache

An erect weed with a stiff stem and toothed leaves both dusty grey. Cultivated land or waste places. Up to 90cm tall. Aug-Sept.

Close-up
of flower

🡔 Nettle

The toothed leaves are covered with stinging hairs. Dangling green-brown flowers. Used to make beer and tea. Common. Up to 100cm tall. June-Aug.

➡ Good King Henry

An erect plant with arrow-shaped leaves and spikes of tiny, green flowers. Farmyards and roadsides. 30-50cm tall. May-July.

Close-up of seed pod

Close-up of flower

⬅ Shepherd's purse

Very common plant. The white flowers and heart-shaped seed pods can be seen all year round. Waysides and waste places. Up to 40cm tall.

Rosette of leaves

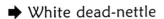

➡ White dead-nettle

Looks like nettle, but the hairs do not sting. Flowers in whorls on the stem. Hedgerows and waste places. Up to 60cm tall. May-Dec.

Note the "hoods" on the flowers

White and green flowers

➡ Bladder campion

Oval leaves in opposite pairs. The sepals are joined together, forming a bladder. Grassy places and hedgerows. 30cm tall. June-Sept.

Calyx is smaller than that of bladder campion

When flowering is over, fruit grows inside sepals (calyx)

⬅ White campion

The erect stems and the sepals are sticky and hairy. The white petals are divided. Look in hedgerows. Up to 100cm tall. May-June.

➡ Corn spurrey

Spindly plant with jointed, sticky stems. Narrow leaves in whorls around the stem. Weed of cornfields. 30cm tall. April-July.

Whorl of leaves

⬅ Chickweed

Mat-forming plant with stems that can grow up to 40cm tall. You can see the small flowers all year round. Common weed in fields and gardens.

➡ Black nightshade

Shrubby weed of cultivated ground. Shiny, oval leaves. Petals fold back to show yellow anthers. The berries are poisonous. 20cm tall. July-Sept.

Anthers

Berries

Whorl of leaves

Fruit

⬅ Goosegrass or common cleavers

Scrambling plant. The prickly stems stick to clothes and animal fur. Hedges. 60cm tall. June-Sept.

White and green flowers

Look for these flowers in grassy places, on waste or cultivated ground.

Anthers

➥ Ribwort plantain or cocks and hens

Tough plant with narrow, ribbed leaves. Green-brown spikes of flowers have white anthers. Common. 20cm tall. April-Aug.

Anthers

Anthers are mauve at first, changing to yellow

➡ Greater plantain or ratstail

Broad-ribbed leaves in a rosette close to the ground. All kinds of cultivated land. 15cm tall. May-Sept.

Anthers

⬅ Hoary plantain

Rosette plant with oval, ribbed leaves. Fine hairs on stem. White flowers have purple anthers. Common in grassy places. 7-15cm tall. May-Aug.

Look for these flowers on grassy or waste ground.

← Yarrow

Common plant with rough stem and feathery leaves. Flat-topped clusters of flowers. Smells sweet. Was once used to heal wounds. 40cm tall. June-Aug.

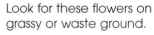

→ Wild chamomile or scented mayweed

Erect plant with finely divided leaves. The petals fold back. Waste places everywhere. 15-40cm tall. June-July.

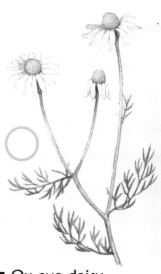

← Ox-eye daisy or marguerite

Erect plant with rosette of toothed leaves and large, daisy-like flowers. Roadsides and grassy places. Up to 60cm tall. June-Aug.

White and green flowers

➡ Starry saxifrage

A rosette plant with shiny, fleshy, toothed leaves. Mountain rocks. 20cm tall. June-Aug.

➡ Meadow saxifrage

Downy, lobed leaves. Up to 40cm tall. Grassy places.

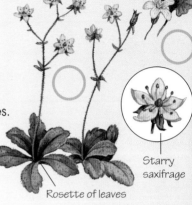

Meadow saxifrage

Starry saxifrage

Rosette of leaves

Seed pods

⬅ Alpine rock cress

Short, mat-forming plant with rosette of greyish-green leaves. Dense clusters of white flowers. Rocks on hills and mountains. April-June.

Close-up of flower

➡ Pellitory-of-the-wall

Plant with red stems and soft hairs. Tiny, stalkless green flowers. Cracks in rocks and walls, and hedgebanks. Up to 100cm tall. June-Oct.

Freshwater flowers

These flowers can be found in or near fresh water, such as streams and ponds.

➡ Meadowsweet

Clusters of sweet-smelling flowers. Grows in marshes, water meadows and also near ditches at the side of the road. Up to 80cm tall. May-Sept.

Undersides of leaves are silvery-grey

The flower stem is three-sided

⬅ Triangular-stalked garlic or three-cornered leek

Smells of garlic. Drooping flowers. In damp hedges and waste places. 40cm tall. June-July.

➡ Floating water plantain

Water plant with oval leaves and white flowers on the water surface. Look for it in canals and still water. Flowers 1-1.5cm across. May-Aug.

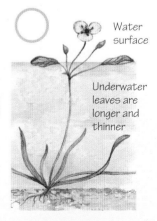

Water surface

Underwater leaves are longer and thinner

Freshwater flowers

➡ Water crowfoot

Water plant whose roots are anchored in the mud at the bottom of ponds and streams. Flowers (1-2cm across) cover the water surface. May-June.

These leaves are on the water surface

Fine, underwater leaves

⬅ Water soldier

Under water except when it flowers. Long, saw-like leaves then show above the surface. Flowers 3-4cm across. Ponds, canals, ditches. June-Aug.

➡ Frogbit

Rises to the surface in spring, and spreads with long runners. Shiny, round leaves grow in tufts. Flowers 2cm across. Canals and ponds. July-Aug.

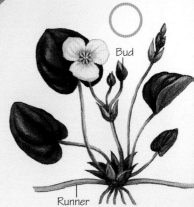

Bud

Runner

Floating-leaved plants

➡ Broad-leaved pondweed

Common in shallow pools of
acid water. Oval floating leaves
and thin, delicate underwater
leaves. Spikes of green
flowers. Up to 1m tall.
June-Aug.

Floating leaves

⬅ Arrowhead

Long, narrow underwater leaves
grow in spring, followed by oval
floating leaves and large upper
leaves like arrowheads. In muddy
water. Up to 1m tall. June-Aug.

➡ Yellow water-lily

Glossy floating leaves
look like blunt, rounded
arrowheads. Seedheads
shaped like light bulbs.
Yellow flowers about
7cm across. June-Aug.

Seedhead

➡ White water-lily

Flowers and leaves float
on the surface of the water.
White petals, sometimes
tinged with pink. Flowers up
to 20cm across. June-Aug.

Underwater plants

➡ Canadian pondweed

Introduced into Europe in about 1850. Grows fast and has choked many waterways. Leaves grow in threes on stem. Flowers are rare. Up to 3.5m long. June-Sept.

Delicate leaves grow under water

⬅ Spiked water milfoil

Very common in chalky, still water. Many small invertebrates shelter on the underwater leaves. Slender flower stem grows above water. Up to 3.5m long. June-July.

➡ Water violet

Long stem and feathery leaves are under water. Cluster of flowers rises up to 40cm above the water. Rare. Found in ditches, ponds and lakes. Mainly eastern Britain. May-June.

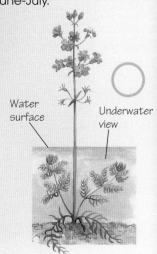

Water surface

Underwater view

← Mare's tail

Narrow leaves, grouped in whorls around stem. Tiny flowers appear at base of leaves. Grows partly submerged in still or slow-moving water. Up to 1m tall. June-July.

→ Water starwort

This water weed is often seen in ditches, streams and ponds. Upper leaves float on the surface in star-shaped clusters. Very small flowers at base of the leaves. Up to 50cm long. May-Sept.

Star-shaped cluster of leaves

Tiny flowers

Anchored to the mud by colourless threads

← Stonewort

This plant does not have flowers. It is found in chalky or salty water. It is brittle and snaps easily. Eaten by ducks. Up to 20cm long.

Seashore flowers

➡ **Thrift or sea pink (left)**

Grows in thick, cushiony
tufts on rocky cliffs.
15cm tall. March-Sept.

➡ **Sea mayweed
(right)**

May be creeping or
upright. Feathery leaves.
Daisy-like flowers. Grows
on cliffs. Up to 60cm tall.
Can be seen in winter.

Thrift or sea pink   Sea mayweed

⬅ **Sea campion**

Common on cliffs and shingle
beaches. Spreads to form cushions
20cm tall. June-August.

Flower
spike

➡ **Buckshorn plantain**

Hairy leaves grow from a point
close to the ground. Look on
gravel near the sea. Spikes of
flowers. 10cm tall. May-Oct.

➡ Annual seablite

May grow along the ground or upright. Fleshy leaves. On saltmarshes in areas of bare mud. 20cm tall.

Downy leaves

Sea milkwort · Sea arrowgrass

⬅ Sea milkwort (left)

Creeping plant that spreads over grassy saltmarshes. June-August.

⬅ Sea arrowgrass (right)

Tough plant with flat, sharp leaves. Grassy saltmarshes. 15-50cm tall. May-Sept.

➡ Sea lavender (left)

Tough, woody plant with leaves in a clump near the ground. Muddy saltmarshes. Up to 40cm tall. July-Sept.

➡ Sea aster (right)

Flowers in late summer, with lilac or white petals. Saltmarshes. Up to 1m tall.

Sea lavender · Sea aster

Seashore flowers

← Sea holly

Prickly plant with clusters of tiny flowers, which attract butterflies. Its thick leaves turn white in winter. Sand and shingle. Up to 50cm tall.

➡ Sea wormwood (left)

Strong-smelling plant. Leaves are downy and greyish green. Grows above high tide level in estuaries. Up to 50cm tall.

➡ Sea purslane (middle)

Grows on edges of deep channels in saltmarshes. 60cm tall. June-Oct.

➡ Marram grass (right)

Common on sand dunes. Its long roots and leaves trap sand and stop it blowing away. Up to 1.2m tall. July-August.

Flower spike

Beware of sharp leaves

Sea wormwood

Sea purslane

Marram grass

← Sea bindweed

Trailing plant with thick, shiny leaves. Can be seen on sand dunes and sometimes on shingle. June-Sept.

88

➡ Yellow horned poppy

Called horned because of the long, green pods which appear in summer. Shingle beaches. Up to 1m tall. June-Sept.

⬅ Sea kale

Grows in clumps on shingle. Broad, fleshy leaves have crinkly edges. Up to 1m tall. June-August.

➡ Golden samphire

Sturdy plant with shiny, fleshy leaves. Often grows in large clumps on saltmarshes, shingle and cliffs. Flowers in autumn. 60cm tall.

⬅ Sea sandwort

Common creeping plant on loose sand and shingle. Helps to stop sand drifting. 30cm tall. May-August.

Trees

Conifers

⬇ Scots pine

Short, blue-green, needles in pairs, and small pointed buds. The bark is red at the top of the tree, and grey and furrowed below. The young tree has a pointed shape, becoming flat-topped with age.

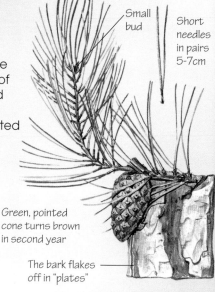

Small bud

Short needles in pairs 5-7cm

Green, pointed cone turns brown in second year

The bark flakes off in "plates"

Long bare trunk is red near top of tree

35m

⬇ Maritime pine

Long, stout, grey-green needles in pairs; long spindle-shaped buds; and long, shiny brown cones grouped in clusters. Rugged bark on a long, bare trunk.

Long needles in pairs 15-20cm

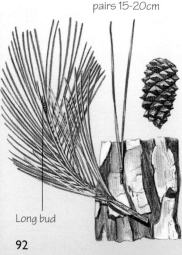

Cones stay on tree for several years

Long bud

22m

92

Green cones turn brown with age.

Paired needles 12-15cm

20m

↑ Stone pine

Umbrella-shaped tree with a flat top, found on the Mediterranean coast. Long dark-green, paired needles, small buds, and broad cones with edible seeds.

Young shoot

Prickly scales

23m

Paired needles 4-5cm

↑ Shore pine

Tall, narrow, fast-growing, with small cones in clusters. Yellow-green needles in pairs on twisted shoots, scaly bark, and sticky, bullet-shaped buds.

Conifers

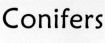

Branches grow at regular intervals

36m

↟ Corsican pine

Tall, fast-growing Mediterranean tree, found on rocky hillsides. Long, dark-green, paired needles; onion-shaped buds; and large lop-sided brown cones. Blackish bark.

Paired needles 12-18cm

Cones take two years to ripen

Young shoot

Paired needles

Shiny, reddish cones stay on tree for many years

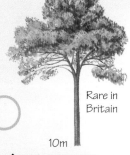

Rare in Britain

10m

↟ Aleppo pine

Small, round-topped Mediterranean tree, with bright-green, paired needles and small round buds. Its cones usually come in groups of two or three.

94

Lower branches sometimes touch the ground

Found in the Alps and other mountainous areas

Needles in fives 7-9cm

17m

⬆ Swiss stone pine

Small, cone-shaped tree, with dense, stiff needles that come in fives. Small, pointed, sticky buds and egg-shaped cones, with edible seeds that ripen and fall in their third year.

Bark is rugged and scaly

Needles in threes – about 10cm

Large, pointed sticky buds

⬇ Monterey pine

Slender, grass-green needles in threes. Large, pointed, sticky buds and squat cones growing flat against the branches, staying on the tree for many years.

Cones uneven at base

30m

Conifers

Needles
1-2cm

Cone scales are
tightly closed

30m

⬆ **Norway spruce**

Traditional Christmas tree.
Regular conical shape, with
prickly dark-green needles,
and cones which hang down.
Leaves peg-like bumps on the
twigs when the needles are
pulled off.

Cones have
papery scales
with crinkled
edges

Needles
2-3cm

35m

⬆ **Sitka spruce**

Narrow cone-shaped
tree, with prickly blue-
green needles and fat
yellow buds. Small knobs
left on yellow twigs when
needles are pulled off.

Grey, scaly bark
flakes off in "plates"

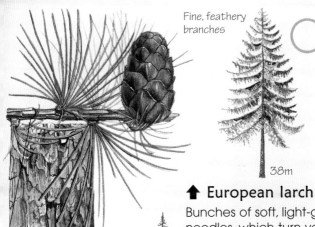

Fine, feathery branches

Straw-coloured twigs

Bare tree in winter

38m

⬆ European larch

Bunches of soft, light-green needles, which turn yellow and fall in winter, leaving small barrel-like knobs on twigs. Small, egg-shaped cones and reddish female flowers.

⬇ Japanese larch

Bunches of blue-green needles, which fall in winter, leaving orange twigs. Pinkish-green female flowers and small, flower-like cones.

Edges of scales turn backwards

The tree has thick branches

35m

Bare tree in winter

97

Conifers

Young cones are green, turning plum-coloured with age

25m

⬆ Nootka cypress

Fern-like sprays of dull green, scale-like leaves grow on either side of the twigs. Plum-coloured cones have prickles on their scales. Cone-shaped crown.

Cone

⬇ European silver fir

Flat single needles, green above and silvery below. Flat, round scars left on twigs when needles drop. Cones shed their scales when ripe, leaving a brown spike.

Large, upright cones

Bracts showing

Rare in Britain, but common in central Europe

Very tall, narrow tree

The twigs are smooth and the needles have notched tips

40m

The needles have pointed tips

30m

⬆ Greek fir

Shiny green, spiny-tipped needles all around twig. Tall, narrow cones shed scales to leave bare spikes on tree. Found only in parks in Britain.

Bark flakes off in "plates"

⬇ Spanish fir

Short, blunt, blue-grey needles all around twig. Cylindrical, upright cones, which shed scales when ripe, like the European silver fir.

The needles have blunt tips

The tree has a conical shape

28m

Conifers

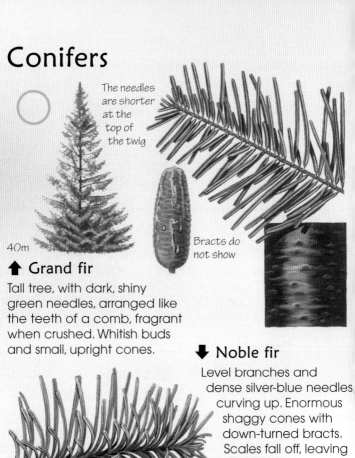

The needles are shorter at the top of the twig

Bracts do not show

40m

⬆ Grand fir

Tall tree, with dark, shiny green needles, arranged like the teeth of a comb, fragrant when crushed. Whitish buds and small, upright cones.

⬇ Noble fir

Level branches and dense silver-blue needles curving up. Enormous shaggy cones with down-turned bracts. Scales fall off, leaving tall spikes.

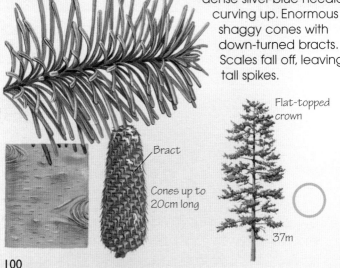

Bract

Cones up to 20cm long

Flat-topped crown

37m

⬆ Douglas fir

Soft, scented needles,
copper-brown buds with
long points, and light-
brown hanging cones
with three-pointed
bracts. Its bark is thick
and grooved when old.

Bract

⬇ Western hemlock

Smooth, brown scaly
bark, drooping branch tips
and top shoots with small
cones. Needles of various
lengths, green above
and silver below.

Tips of
branches
droop

Older cones
are brown

Flattened needles

Young cones
are green

35m

40m

Conifers

⬇ Western red cedar

Small, flower-shaped
cones and smooth,
finely furrowed bark.
The twigs are covered
with flattened sprays
of scented,
scale-like
leaves.

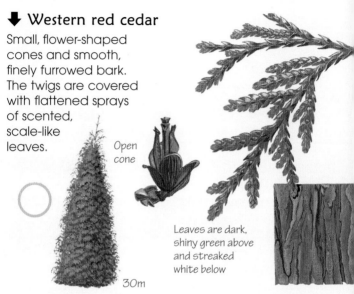

Open
cone

Leaves are dark,
shiny green above
and streaked
white below

30m

⬇ Lawson cypress

Sprays of fine, scale-like
leaves, green and other
colours. Small, round cones
and smooth, reddish bark.
The leader shoot (at tree
top) often droops.

Small
cones

Spray of
scale-like
leaves

25m

102

Cones are shiny pale-green at first, dull grey when older

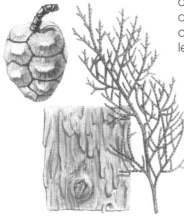

⬇ Italian cypress

An upright, narrow crowned, mainly ornamental tree. Small, dark, dull-green, scale-like leaves, closely pressed to stem. Large, rounded cones.

Leaves are smaller than Monterey cypress (below)

15m

⬇ Monterey cypress

Dense sprays of small, scale-like leaves and large, purplish-brown, rounded cones with knobs on scales. Column-shaped, becoming flat-topped when old, and the bark is often peeling.

Leaves are lemon-scented when crushed

25m

Peeling bark

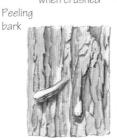

Knob

Conifers

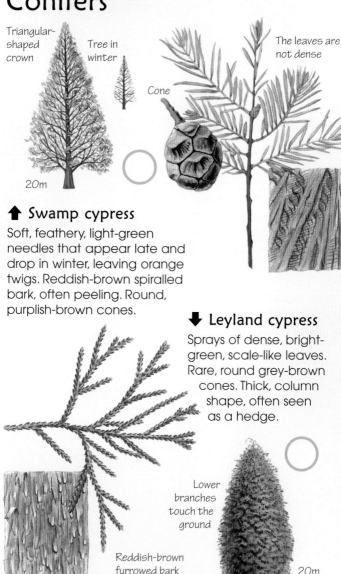

Triangular-shaped crown

Tree in winter

Cone

The leaves are not dense

20m

⬆ Swamp cypress

Soft, feathery, light-green needles that appear late and drop in winter, leaving orange twigs. Reddish-brown spiralled bark, often peeling. Round, purplish-brown cones.

⬇ Leyland cypress

Sprays of dense, bright-green, scale-like leaves. Rare, round grey-brown cones. Thick, column shape, often seen as a hedge.

Lower branches touch the ground

Reddish-brown furrowed bark

20m

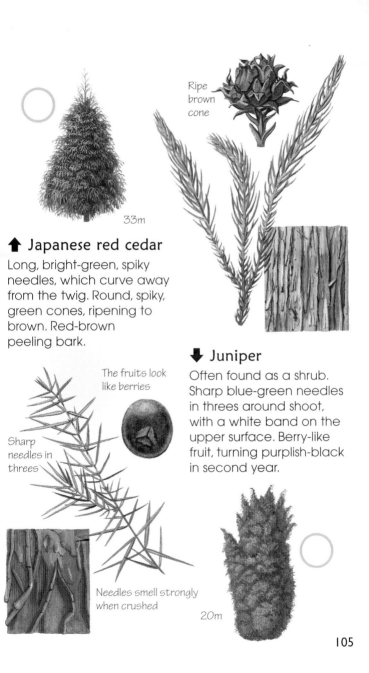

⬆ Japanese red cedar

Long, bright-green, spiky needles, which curve away from the twig. Round, spiky, green cones, ripening to brown. Red-brown peeling bark.

33m

Ripe brown cone

⬇ Juniper

Often found as a shrub. Sharp blue-green needles in threes around shoot, with a white band on the upper surface. Berry-like fruit, turning purplish-black in second year.

The fruits look like berries

Sharp needles in threes

Needles smell strongly when crushed

20m

105

Conifers

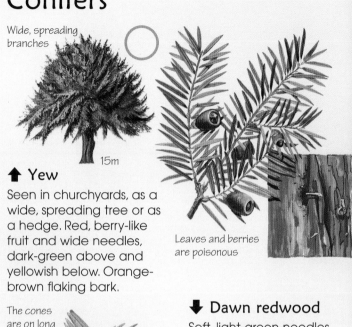

Wide, spreading branches

15m

Leaves and berries are poisonous

⬆ Yew

Seen in churchyards, as a wide, spreading tree or as a hedge. Red, berry-like fruit and wide needles, dark-green above and yellowish below. Orange-brown flaking bark.

The cones are on long stalks, but rare

⬇ Dawn redwood

Soft, light-green needles, similar to the swamp cypress (see page 104), but larger, turning reddish in autumn. Bark is orange in young trees, flaking and furrowed in older ones.

The needles turn reddish in autumn

Bare tree in winter

20m

Needles parted on either side of the twig

↓ Coast redwood

Tall tree, with thick, reddish, spongy bark. Hard, sharp-pointed, single needles, dark-green above and white-banded below. Small, round cones.

33m

↓ Wellingtonia

Tall, with soft, thick, deeply furrowed bark. Deep-green, scale-like, pointed leaves, hanging from upswept branches. Long-stalked, round, corky cones. Also called giant sequoia.

Foliage hanging from upswept branches

38m

Diamond-shaped cone scales wrinkle when they ripen

Conifers

⬇ Atlas cedar

Large, spreading tree with dark-green needles, in bunches on the older shoots. Large, barrel-shaped, upright cones with sunken tops.

Sunken top

Leaves are blue-green in the common garden variety, dark green in the wild

25m

Top not sunken

Cones are covered with sticky resin

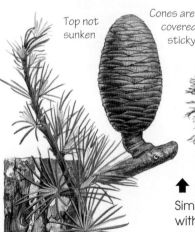

30m

⬆ Cedar of Lebanon

Similar to Atlas cedar, but without sunken tops on cones. Branches spread out into level, leafy platforms.

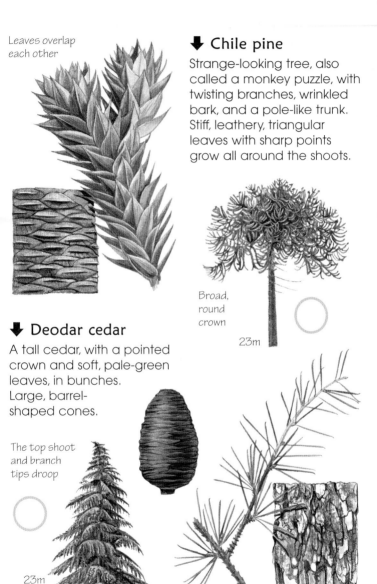

Leaves overlap each other

⬇ Chile pine

Strange-looking tree, also called a monkey puzzle, with twisting branches, wrinkled bark, and a pole-like trunk. Stiff, leathery, triangular leaves with sharp points grow all around the shoots.

Broad, round crown

23m

⬇ Deodar cedar

A tall cedar, with a pointed crown and soft, pale-green leaves, in bunches. Large, barrel-shaped cones.

The top shoot and branch tips droop

23m

Broadleaved trees

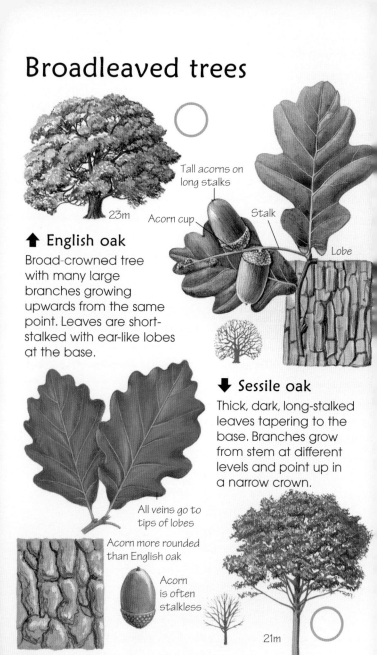

Tall acorns on long stalks

Acorn cup

Stalk

Lobe

23m

⬆ English oak

Broad-crowned tree with many large branches growing upwards from the same point. Leaves are short-stalked with ear-like lobes at the base.

⬇ Sessile oak

Thick, dark, long-stalked leaves tapering to the base. Branches grow from stem at different levels and point up in a narrow crown.

All veins go to tips of lobes

Acorn more rounded than English oak

Acorn is often stalkless

21m

↓ Holm oak

Ornamental tree with a broad dense crown. Shiny, evergreen leaves, greyish-green beneath, sometimes with shallow teeth like holly.

Evergreen leaves

Teeth

Small acorn, almost covered by cup

20m

↓ Turkey oak

Leaves unevenly lobed. Whiskers on buds and at base of leaves. Acorns ripen in second autumn. Acorn cups mossy and stalkless.

Acorn cup is mossy

25m

Broadleaved trees

16m

Twisted trunk
and branches

Cork is obtained
from the bark

Acorn

⬆ Cork oak

Common in southern Europe,
but extremely rare in Britain.
Smaller than other oaks, it has
thick, corky, whitish bark and
shiny, evergreen leaves with
wavy edges.

⬇ Red oak

Smooth, silvery bark, and
squat acorns in shallow
cups that ripen in second
year. Large leaves, with
bristly-tipped lobes, turn
reddish brown in autumn.

The leaves turn
reddish in
autumn

Acorn

20m

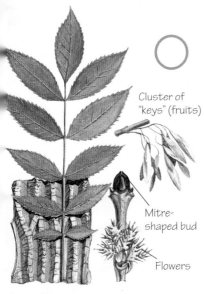

Cluster of
"keys" (fruits)

Mitre-
shaped bud

Flowers

⬆ Common ash

Pale-grey bark and
compound leaves of
9-13 leaflets, appearing
late, after bunches of
purplish flowers. Clusters
of seeds stay on the
tree into winter.

25m

⬇ Manna ash

Smooth grey bark oozing
a sugary liquid called
manna. Leaves of 5-9
stalked leaflets appear
with clusters of white
flowers in May.

20m

Fruit

Flowers

Leaflets downy
near veins

113

Broadleaved trees

Leaf has notched tip

12m

Ripe brown, woody cone

⬆ Common alder

Rounded leaves fall in late autumn, reddish catkins and small, brown, woody cones. Sticky young twigs and leaves. Often found near water.

⬇ Grey alder

Fast-growing, with catkins and fruit like the common alder. Pointed oval leaves, with sharply-toothed, edges, soft and grey beneath.

These green fruits ripen into brown, woody "cones"

14m

Flower
(from a
cluster)

Leaves with
toothed
edges

7m

⬆ Rowan

Often grows alone on
mountainsides; also known as
mountain ash. Tooth-edged
compound leaves, smaller
than other ashes. Clusters of
creamy-white flowers in May,
and red berries in August.

Leaves turn red
in the autumn

⬇ Whitebeam

Flowers and berries similar
to rowan, but ripening
later. Large oval leaves,
with toothed edges, dark-
green above, white and
furry underneath.

Berries

8m

Broadleaved trees

Leaf stalks are long and flattened

⬆ Aspen

Rounded leaves with wavy edges, deep-green on top, paler beneath. White downy catkins. Grey bark with large irregular markings. Often found growing in thickets.

⬇ Black Italian poplar

Dark-green, triangular, pointed leaves appearing late. Red catkins and deeply furrowed bark. Trunk and crown often lean away from the wind.

25m

20m

Lower leaves are less lobed

Wavy edges

Underside of leaf

Diamond-shaped marks on young bark

↑ White poplar

Five-lobed leaves, downy white underneath, so the crown looks white. Lower bark is dark and rugged; upper bark, pale grey, with diamond shapes on young trees. Tree often leans slightly.

20m

↓ Western balsam poplar

Large, triangular, pointed leaves, very pale underneath. Sticky and sweet-smelling buds and young leaves. Long purplish catkins and white fluffy seeds.

Underside of leaf

35m

117

Broadleaved trees

Leaf shape varies slightly

28m

↑ Lombardy poplar
Tall, narrow tree, often found along roadsides on the European continent. Pointed, triangular leaves, furrowed bark, and branches that grow upwards from the ground.

15m

↑ Silver birch
Slender tree with silvery bark and drooping branches. Small, diamond-shaped leaves, with toothed edges, and long "lamb's tail" catkins in April.

Catkin

Silvery bark peels off in ribbons

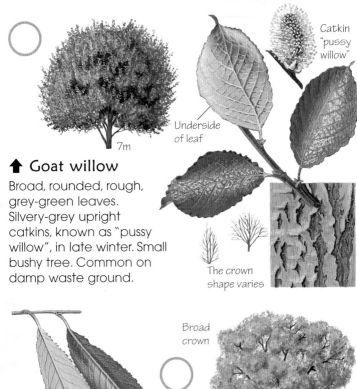

⬆ Goat willow

Broad, rounded, rough, grey-green leaves. Silvery-grey upright catkins, known as "pussy willow", in late winter. Small bushy tree. Common on damp waste ground.

Catkin "pussy willow"

Underside of leaf

The crown shape varies

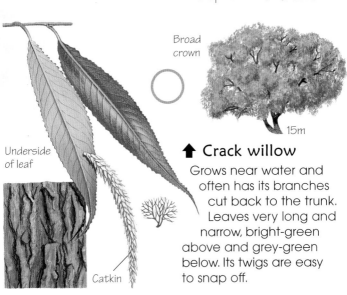

Broad crown

Underside of leaf

Catkin

⬆ Crack willow

Grows near water and often has its branches cut back to the trunk. Leaves very long and narrow, bright-green above and grey-green below. Its twigs are easy to snap off.

Broadleaved trees

Underside of leaf

Catkin

20m

⬆ White willow

Found by streams and rivers. Long, narrow, finely toothed leaves, white underneath. Slender twigs that are hard to break. One variety with trailing branches is known as weeping willow.

Leaves on short stalks

Fruits

20m

⬆ Southern beech

Triangular-shaped crown, and narrow, oval leaves, with fine-toothed edges and many obvious veins. Deep-green, prickly fruit, and silver-grey bark.

Leaves are wavy-edged

Husk

Nut

↑ Common beech

Tall tree with a spreading crown. Light-green, oval leaves that turn copper brown in autumn. Smooth grey bark, and triangular nuts with hairy husks.

25m

↑ Hornbeam

Sharply toothed, oval leaves. In autumn, clusters of three-pronged, leaf-like wings hold nuts. Smooth, grey bark is fluted or rippled.

10m

Cluster of green winged fruits

Broadleaved trees

⬇ Crab apple

Small, bushy tree, found in hedges. Small, rounded leaves with toothed edges. Pinkish-white flowers in May. Small, sour, speckled reddish-green apples that can be used in cooking.

Apple tastes sour even when ripe

10m

⬇ Common pear

Found in woods and hedgerows. Large, white flowers in April. Small pears that are gritty to eat. Small, dark-green leaves, with finely toothed edges and long stalks.

Pear is golden when ripe

15m

↑ Blackthorn

Small tree, with oval leaves. Foamy, white flowers on bare twigs in March. Small, blue-black fruit, called sloes, in September.

5m

Berries called haws

8m

↑ Hawthorn

Shiny, deeply lobed, dark-green leaves and thorny twigs. Clusters of small, white flowers in May, and dark-red berries. Rounded crown.

Broadleaved trees

↑ London plane

Large, broad leaves in pairs, with pointed lobes. Spiny "bobble" fruits hang all winter. Flaking bark, leaving yellowish patches. Often found in towns.

Fruit

Leaves have toothed edges

↑ Sycamore

Large spreading tree, with dark-green leathery leaves with toothed edges and five lobes. Paired, right-angled, winged fruits. Smooth brown bark, becoming scaly.

Fruits twist as they fall

Pairs of fruits
spin as they fall

↑ Norway maple

Light-green, thin leaves,
with bristle-tipped lobes
and teeth. Wide-angled,
paired fruits and finely
furrowed, grey bark.

15m

Lobes
are blunt

Leaves
turn golden
in autumn

10m

↑ Field maple

Small, round-headed
tree, often found in
hedges. Small, dark-
green leaves with five
lobes, and small, reddish,
winged fruits.

Fruits

125

Broadleaved trees

Broad crown

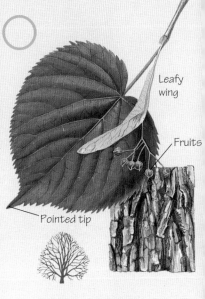

Leafy wing

Fruits

Pointed tip

25m

⬆ Common lime

Heart-shaped leaves
with toothed edges.
Yellowish-green,
scented flowers in July.
Small, round, hard,
grey-green fruits hang
from a leafy wing.

⬇ Silver lime

Like the common lime,
but with a more rounded
crown. Dark-green leaves,
silvery-grey below. Fruits
hang from a leafy wing.

Leafy wing

Fruits

Rounded crown

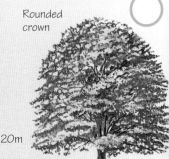

20m

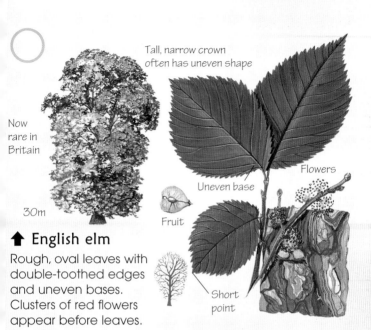

Tall, narrow crown often has uneven shape

Now rare in Britain

30m

Flowers

Uneven base

Fruit

Short point

⬆ English elm

Rough, oval leaves with double-toothed edges and uneven bases. Clusters of red flowers appear before leaves.

⬇ Wych elm

Like the English elm, but with a round, even crown; larger, rougher, stalkless leaves; and larger seeds. Now very rare in Britain.

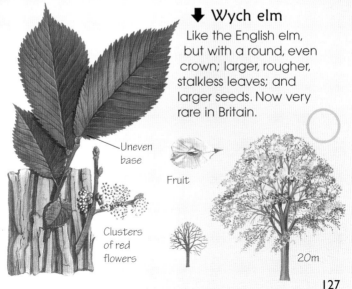

Uneven base

Fruit

Clusters of red flowers

20m

Broadleaved trees

⬇ Horse chestnut

Brown, inedible "conkers" in green, spiny cases. Compound leaves of 5-7 large leaflets. "Candles" of white or pink flowers in May.

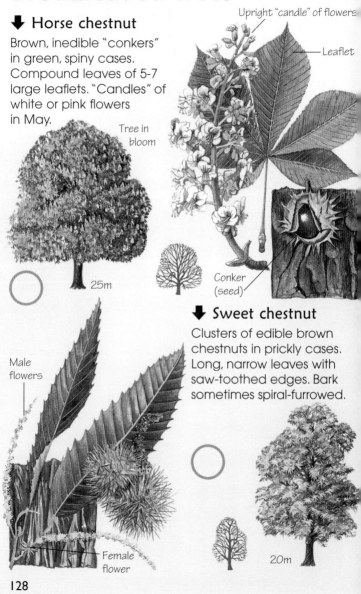

Upright "candle" of flowers

Leaflet

Tree in bloom

25m

Conker (seed)

⬇ Sweet chestnut

Clusters of edible brown chestnuts in prickly cases. Long, narrow leaves with saw-toothed edges. Bark sometimes spiral-furrowed.

Male flowers

Female flower

20m

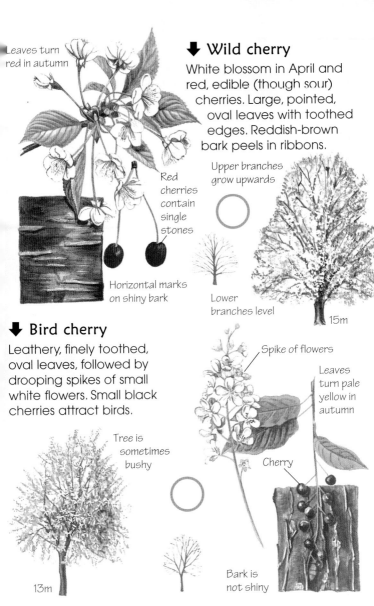

Leaves turn red in autumn

⬇ Wild cherry

White blossom in April and red, edible (though sour) cherries. Large, pointed, oval leaves with toothed edges. Reddish-brown bark peels in ribbons.

Red cherries contain single stones

Upper branches grow upwards

Horizontal marks on shiny bark

Lower branches level

15m

⬇ Bird cherry

Leathery, finely toothed, oval leaves, followed by drooping spikes of small white flowers. Small black cherries attract birds.

Tree is sometimes bushy

Spike of flowers

Leaves turn pale yellow in autumn

Cherry

13m

Bark is not shiny

129

Broadleaved trees

25m

Unripe fruit

Ripe fruit

Young fruits

⬆ Black mulberry

Rough, heart-shaped leaves with toothed edges. Blackish-red berries. Short trunk, twisted branches. Flowers in short spikes.

Smooth, green case containing edible walnut

Young fruit

⬇ Common walnut

Broad crown. Smooth, grey bark, with some cracks. Compound leaves of seven to nine leaflets, and hollow twigs.

Leaves are bronze when they first open, turning green later

20m

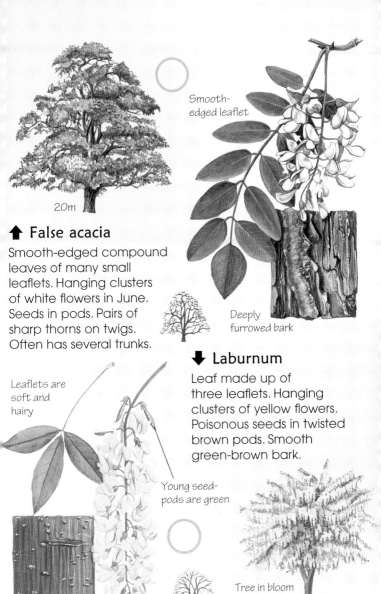

Smooth-edged leaflet

↑ False acacia

Smooth-edged compound leaves of many small leaflets. Hanging clusters of white flowers in June. Seeds in pods. Pairs of sharp thorns on twigs. Often has several trunks.

20m

Deeply furrowed bark

↓ Laburnum

Leaf made up of three leaflets. Hanging clusters of yellow flowers. Poisonous seeds in twisted brown pods. Smooth green-brown bark.

Leaflets are soft and hairy

Young seed-pods are green

Tree in bloom (May-June) 7m

Broadleaved trees

⬇ Holly

Small tree with shiny, dark, evergreen leaves with thorny prickles. Small, white flowers. Round red berries. Smooth grey-green bark.

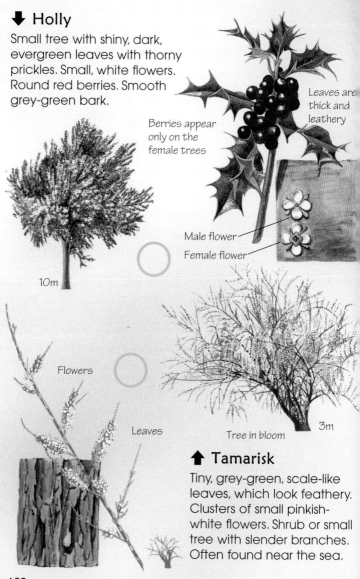

Leaves are thick and leathery

Berries appear only on the female trees

10m

Male flower

Female flower

Flowers

Leaves

Tree in bloom

3m

⬆ Tamarisk

Tiny, grey-green, scale-like leaves, which look feathery. Clusters of small pinkish-white flowers. Shrub or small tree with slender branches. Often found near the sea.

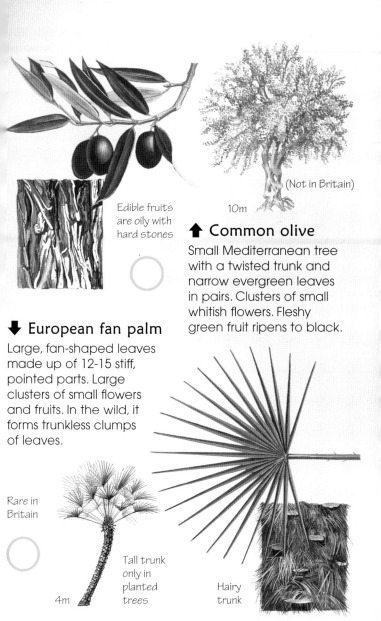

Edible fruits
are oily with
hard stones

(Not in Britain)

10m

⬆ Common olive

Small Mediterranean tree
with a twisted trunk and
narrow evergreen leaves
in pairs. Clusters of small
whitish flowers. Fleshy
green fruit ripens to black.

⬇ European fan palm

Large, fan-shaped leaves
made up of 12-15 stiff,
pointed parts. Large
clusters of small flowers
and fruits. In the wild, it
forms trunkless clumps
of leaves.

Rare in
Britain

Tall trunk
only in
planted
trees

4m

Hairy
trunk

Broadleaved trees

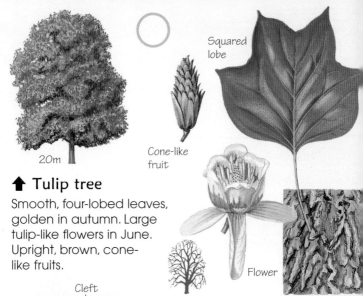

Squared lobe

Cone-like fruit

⬆ Tulip tree

Smooth, four-lobed leaves, golden in autumn. Large tulip-like flowers in June. Upright, brown, cone-like fruits.

20m

Flower

Cleft

⬇ Maidenhair tree

Tall, slender tree. Double-lobed, fan-shaped leaves with deep cleft, bright yellow in autumn. Female trees have hanging fruit, but male trees are more common.

Maidenhair tree is neither a conifer nor a broadleaved tree. It is in a group on its own.

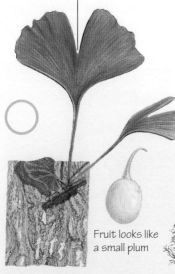

Fruit looks like a small plum

23m

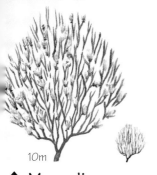

↑ Magnolia

Wide, spreading tree.
Large white flowers on
naked twigs in March,
before large, smooth,
dark-green, oval leaves.

*Winged fruits ripen from
green to reddish-brown*

*Smooth grey-brown
bark with white streaks*

22m

↑ Tree of Heaven

Large compound leaves
made up of 5-20 pairs
of stalked leaflets. Large
clusters of greenish flowers
in July, followed by clusters
of winged fruits.

Birds

Geese

➡ Brent goose

Look for this small, dark goose on estuaries in winter. 58cm.

Canada geese were brought here from North America

Brent goose

⬅ Canada goose

A large, noisy goose. Look in parks. Nests wild in Britain. 95cm.

➡ Greylag goose

Nests wild in Scotland and others have been released further south. Wild birds from Iceland visit Scotland in winter. 82cm.

⬅ Barnacle goose

Look for barnacle geese on the west coasts of Britain and Ireland in winter. Feeds in flocks on farmland. 63cm.

Barnacle goose has more white on head than Canada goose

Geese, swans

➡ Pink-footed goose

A winter visitor. Seen
in large numbers on
fields in Scotland
and near coasts in
England. 68cm.

⬅ Bean goose

A rare winter visitor from
northern Europe. Grazes
on farmland away from
the coast. 80cm.

➡ White-fronted goose

A winter visitor to estuaries,
marshes and farmland.
Look for white at base
of bill. 72cm.

Mute
swan
152cm

Whooper
swan
152cm

Bewick's
swan
122cm

⬅ Swans

Mute swans are often
seen in parks or on
rivers. The others come
to Britain in winter and
can be seen on lakes
or flooded fields.

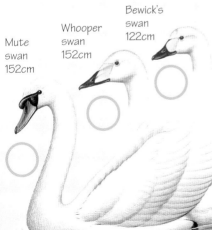

139

Ducks

Mallard Teal Wigeon

♀

♂

← Mallard

Found near most inland waters. Only the female gives the familiar "quack". 58cm.

→ Teal

Smallest European duck. A very shy bird. It prefers the shallow edges of lakes. Flies with fast wing-beats. 35cm.

♀

♂

← Wigeon

Sometimes seen grazing on fields near water. Forms flocks in winter especially near the sea. Male's call is a loud "wheeo". 46cm.

♀

♂

→ Pintail

Uses its long neck to feed on plants under the water. Look for these birds in winter, often near sea. 66cm.

♀

♂

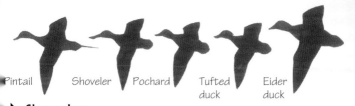

Pintail   Shoveler   Pochard   Tufted duck   Eider duck

➡ Shoveler

Likes quiet lakes and shallow water. Uses its long, flat bill to filter food from the surface of the water. Call is low "quack". 51cm.

♀

♂

♀

♂

⬅ Pochard

Spends much of its time resting on open water and diving for food. More likely to be seen in winter. 46cm.

➡ Tufted duck

Another diving duck which is more common in winter. Can sometimes be seen on park lakes. 43cm.

♀

♂

♀

♂

⬅ Eider

Breeds around rocky northern coasts. Forms large flocks on the sea in winter. 58cm.

Ducks

➡ Goldeneye

A few nest in Scotland, but mainly a winter visitor from northern Europe. Seen on the sea and inland lakes, often in small flocks. Dives frequently. 46cm.

⬅ Red-breasted merganser

Breeds by lakes and rivers. Seldom seen inland in winter, but visits many coastal areas and open sea. Dives for fish. 58cm.

➡ Goosander

Most British goosanders nest in the north and west. Likes large lakes in winter. Dives for fish. Look for shaggy crest on female. 66cm.

⬅ Shelduck

Common around most sandy coasts, especially estuaries. Often in flocks. Groups of young join together in late summer. Looks slow and heavy in flight. 61cm.

Female has no lump on bill

Grebes, heron, stork

➡ Great crested grebe

Found on inland waters. Dives for fish. Beautiful courtship displays in spring. May be seen on sea in winter. 48cm.

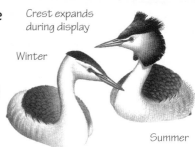

Crest expands during display

Winter

Summer

Winter

Summer

⬅ Little grebe or dabchick

Common on inland waters, but secretive and hard to spot. Call is a shrill trill. 27cm.

➡ Grey heron

Usually seen near water. Nests in colonies in trees. Eats fish, frogs and small mammals. 92cm.

Head drawn back and legs stick out when flying

⬅ White stork

Very rare in Britain. Likes wet areas. Will nest on buildings and pylons in Europe. 102cm.

Rails, crake

➡ Moorhen

A water bird that lives near ponds, lakes or streams. Notice red bill and white tail. Young are brown. 33cm.

⬅ Coot

Dives a lot. Prefers large lakes. Look for white bill and forehead. Young are grey with pale throats and breasts. Flocks in winter. 38cm.

➡ Corncrake

Difficult to see as it lives in long grass. Repeats "crex-crex" cry monotonously, especially after dark. Rare in Britain. 27cm.

⬅ Water rail

Secretive bird that lives in reed beds. Listen for its piglet-like squeal. Legs trail in flight. Swims for short distances. 28cm.

Cormorant, gannet, shag, chough

➡ Cormorant

Seen near the sea but also at inland lakes. Some have grey head and neck in breeding season. Nests in colonies. 92cm.

White patch in breeding season

⬅ Gannet

Look for gannets out to sea, close to waves. Plunges head-first into water to catch fish. 92cm.

Crest only in nesting season

↖ Shag

Lives near the sea. Nests in colonies on rocky coasts. Dives for fish. Young are brown. 78cm.

➡ Chough

A crow which lives on high, rocky sea cliffs and in mountains. Like a jackdaw, but has red feet and red beak. 38cm.

Waders

White collar in winter

← Oystercatcher

Usually seen near the sea, especially in winter. Nests inland in Scotland and parts of England. Feeds on shellfish. 43cm.

Summer

White wing bars show in flight

➡ Lapwing

A farmland bird which flocks in winter. Looks black and white from a distance. Displays in the air in breeding season. Calls "pee-wit". 30cm.

Broad, rounded wings

Summer

← Turnstone

Likes shingle or rocky shores. Turns stones over to find food. Does not nest in Britain, but can be seen most months. 23cm.

Winter

➡ Ringed plover

Usually found near the
sea, but sometimes
by inland lakes. Likes
sandy or shingle
shores. Seen all the
year round. 19cm.

Summer

Juvenile

Broad
white bar
on wing

Adult

Notice
yellow
eye-ring

⬅ Little ringed plover

Summer visitor. Most
common in southeast
England. Likes gravel pits
and shingle banks inland.
Legs are yellowish. 15cm.

Golden plover
in winter

Northern
Europe

Southern
Europe

➡ Golden plover

Breeds on upland
moors, but found
in flocks on coastal
marshes or lowland
farms in winter. 28cm.

Waders

➡ Redshank

Breeds on seashores and wet meadows. Look for white on rump and back edges of wings in flight. 28cm.

Red legs

⬅ Greenshank

Rarer and slightly bigger than redshank. Seen in spring and autumn on coasts or inland. Some nest in northern Scotland. 30cm.

➡ Common sandpiper

Summer visitor to upland streams and lakes. Visits wet areas in lowland Britain in spring and autumn. Wags tail and bobs. 20cm.

Summer

Winter

White wing bar

Summer

⬅ Black-tailed godwit

A few nest in wet meadows in Britain, but more seen on coasts during autumn and winter. 41cm.

➡ Bar-tailed godwit

Smaller than black-tailed godwit. Most are seen in spring and autumn, but some winter on east coast mud flats or estuaries. 37cm.

Winter

Pale rump

No wing bar

⬅ Curlew

Britain's largest wader. Nests on moors and upland farmland. Seen on coasts at other times of year. Song is "courli". 48-64cm.

Look for stripe on head

Bill shorter than curlew's

➡ Whimbrel

Like a small curlew. A few nest in heather in northern Scotland. Many more visit Britain's coasts in spring and autumn. 40cm.

149

Waders

◄ Dunlin

A common visitor to seashores, but nests on moorland in the north. Often seen in flocks. Beak straight or down-curved. 19cm.

Winter

➡ Knot

Seen in huge flocks in winter. Likes sand or mud flats in estuaries. Rare inland. Mainly a winter visitor. Breeds in the Arctic. 25cm.

◄ Sanderling

Seen on coasts in winter. Runs along water's edge on sandy beaches where it catches small animals washed up by waves. 20cm.

Winter

➡ Ruff

Seen in autumn and spring, but also winter in wet places and a few stay to nest. Male 29cm. Female 23cm.

♂

♀

Summer

Winter

150

➤ Woodcock

Secretive bird of damp
woods. Watch out for its
bat-like display flight over
woods at dusk in early
summer. 34cm.

Snipe in flight

Woodcock
in flight

◀ Snipe

Lives in wet fields, marshes
or lake edges. Hard to see
on the ground, but rises up
with a zig-zag flight when
disturbed. 27cm.

➤ Avocet

Nests on coastal
marshes in eastern
England. Flocks winter
on southern estuaries.
Rare inland. 43cm.

151

Gulls

➡ Black-headed gull

Common near the sea
and inland. Nests in
colonies. Look for white
front edge of long
wings. 37cm.

Winter

Dark brown
head in
summer only

⬅ Lesser black-backed gull

Mainly summer visitor
to coasts or inland.
Some winter in Britain.
Head streaked with
grey in winter. 53cm.

Legs yellow
in summer

➡ Great black-backed gull

Britain's largest gull. Not very
common inland. Nests on
rocky coasts. Often solitary.
Legs pinkish. 66cm.

⬅ Common gull

Some nest in Scotland
and Ireland. Seen further
south and often inland in
winter. 41cm.

Gull, terns

Summer

◀ Herring gull

Common in ports and seaside towns. Scrounges food from people and even nests on buildings. Young's plumage is mottled brown for first three years. 56cm.

➡ Arctic tern
➡ Common tern

Both species most likely to be seen near the sea, but common tern also nests inland. Both dive into water to catch fish. 34cm.

Arctic tern in summer

Common tern's bill has black tip

Summer

◀ Black tern

A spring and autumn visitor. Can be seen flying low over lakes, dipping down to pick food from surface. 24cm.

Summer

Autumn

➡ Little tern

Summer visitor. Nests in small groups on shingle beaches. Dives for fish. 24cm.

Yellow bill with black tip

Summer

Auks, fulmar

Neck and throat are white in winter

Summer

◀ Razorbill

Look for its flat-sided bill. Nests on cliffs and rocky shores in colonies. Winters at sea. Dives for fish. Often with guillemots. 41cm.

➡ Guillemot

Nests on cliffs in large groups. Slimmer than razorbill. Northern birds have white eye-ring and line on heads. 42cm.

Neck and throat are white in winter

Summer

◀ Fulmar

Nests in colonies on ledges on sea cliffs. Often glides close to the waves on stiff wings. Can be seen near cliffs all round our coasts. 47cm.

➡ Puffin

Rocky islands and sea cliffs in the north and west. Nests between rocks or in burrows in the ground. 30cm.

Colourful beak and reddish feet in summer

Birds of prey

➡ Hobby

Catches large insects and birds in the air. Summer visitor to southern England. Look on heaths and near water. 33cm.

Tail shorter and wings longer than kestrel

⬅ Goshawk

Looks like a large sparrowhawk. Lives in woods. Rare in Britain. Male 48cm. Female 58cm.

➡ Peregrine

Sea cliffs or inland crags. Hunts over estuaries and marshes in winter. Dives on flying birds at great speed. 38-48cm.

⬅ Honey buzzard

Summer visitor to British woodlands. Eats mainly grubs of wasps and bees. Rare. 51-59cm.

Birds of prey

➡ Osprey

Rare summer visitor to Britain. Some nest in Scotland but seen further south on its migration to Africa. Plunges into water to catch fish. 56cm.

Upper parts are dark brown

Wings narrower than buzzard's

Long, broad wings

⬅ Golden eagle

Lives in Scottish Highlands. Young birds have white on wings and tail. Glides for long distances. Bigger than buzzard. 83cm.

➡ Red kite

This rare bird nests in oak woods in Mid Wales. Recently released in Scotland and England and increasing in numbers. Soars for long periods. 62cm.

Long forked tail

Notice the
pale wing
patches

← Buzzard

Large bird of prey with
broad wings. Often seen
soaring over moors and
farmland as it hunts. Rarer
in southern and eastern
England. 54cm.

Female is
larger and
browner
than male

→ Sparrowhawk

Broad-winged hawk. Hunts
small birds along hedges
and woodland edges.
Never hovers. Male
30cm. Female 38cm.

♀

♂

Long,
pointed
wings and
tail

♀

♂

← Kestrel

Well-known for the way
it hovers when hunting,
especially alongside
motorways. Some nest in
towns. Eats birds, insects
and small mammals. 34cm.

Owls

➡ Barn owl

Its call is an eerie
shriek. Often nests in old
buildings or hollow trees.
Hunts small mammals
and roosting birds
at night. 34cm.

Birds with dark
faces and breasts
are found in north
and east Europe

Bouncing
flight

⬅ Little owl

Small, flat-headed owl.
Flies low over farmland
and hunts at dusk. Nests
in tree-holes. Bobs up and
down when curious. 22cm.

➡ Tawny owl

Calls with familiar "hoot".
Hunts at night where
there are woods or
old trees. Eats small
mammals or birds.
38cm.

⬅ Pygmy owl

The smallest European
owl. Found in mountain
forests, but not in Britain.
Has a whistling "keeoo"
call. Hunts small birds in
flight. 16cm.

➡ Short-eared owl

Hunts small mammals in
daylight and at dusk.
Likes open country.
Perches on the ground.
Fierce-looking. 37cm.

⬅ Long-eared owl

A secretive night-hunting
owl of thick pine woods.
Roosts during the day.
Long "ear" tufts cannot
be seen in flight. 34cm.

➡ Tengmalm's owl

Small owl that lives in northern
and central European forests.
Very rare visitor to Britain.
Hunts at night. Nests in
tree-holes. 25cm.

⬅ Scops owl

Very rare visitor from
southern Europe. Gives
monotonous "kiu" call
from hidden perch.
Hunts only at night. 19cm.

159

Game birds

➤ Red grouse
➤ Willow grouse

Red grouse lives
on moors in Britain.
Willow grouse lives
in northern Europe.
Willow grouse
is white in
winter. 36cm.

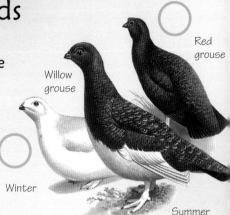

Red
grouse

Willow
grouse

Winter

Summer

In summer, the male's
plumage is browner
and the female's
yellower than
in autumn

Winter

◀ Ptarmigan

Lives on barren mountain
tops in the north. Has
three different plumages
and is well camouflaged.
Allows people to get
close. 34cm.

Autumn

➤ Black grouse

Found on edge of
moorland, sometimes
perched in trees.
Groups of males display
together at an area
known as a "lek".
Male 53cm.
Female 41cm.

♂ ♀

➡ Capercaillie

Lives in pine forests in parts of Scotland. Eats pine shoots at tips of branches. Male 86cm. Female 61cm.

⬅ Grey partridge

Often in small groups. Likes farmland with hedges. Its call is a grating "kirr-ic". Rare in Ireland. 30cm.

➡ Pheasant

Lives on farmland with hedges. Often reared as game. Roosts in trees. Nests on ground. Male 87cm. Female 58cm.

Look for long tail

Males can vary in colour and often have a white neck ring

⬅ Red-legged partridge

Common in southern and eastern Britain. Fields and open sandy areas. Often runs rather than flies. 34cm.

Hoopoe, nightjar, cuckoo, kingfisher

➡ Hoopoe

Rare visitor to Britain, seen mainly in spring. More common in southern Europe. Probes ground for insects with its long bill. 28cm.

⬅ Nightjar

Rarely seen in daylight. Listen for churring call at night when it hunts insects. Summer migrant to heathland. 27cm.

Male has white spots on wings

➡ Cuckoo

Male's song well known. Female has bubbling call. Found all over Britain in summer. Looks like a sparrowhawk in flight. 30cm.

Juvenile cuckoo

⬅ Kingfisher

Small and brilliantly coloured. Seen near lakes and rivers. Dives for fish. Listen for shrill whistle. 17cm.

Usually flies low and straight over water

Woodpeckers

➤ Black woodpecker

Size of a rook. Found in forests in Europe, especially old pine woods, but not in Britain. Can be confused with crow in flight. 46cm.

♂

Male (shown here) has red crown. Female has red patch on back of head.

♀

♂

Large white patches on wings

← Great spotted woodpecker

Size of a blackbird. Found in woods all over Britain. Drums on trees in spring. 23cm.

♂

♀

Stripy back

➤ Lesser spotted woodpecker

Sparrow-sized. Lacks white wing patches of great spotted woodpecker. Male has red crown. Open woodland. Not in Scotland. 14cm.

Yellow-green rump

← Green woodpecker

Pigeon-sized. Often feeds on ground. Open woods and parks. Quite common in England and Wales. Rare in Scotland. Has a laugh-like call. 32cm.

Woodpeckers do not live in Ireland. They all have bouncing flight.

Swift, swallow, martins

➡ Swift

A common migrant that
visits Britain from May
to August. Flies fast over
towns and country, often
in flocks. Listen for its
screaming call. 17cm.

Swift's tail
is forked

Catches
insects
in flight

Swallow's tail
has streamers
when adult

⬅ Swallow

Summer migrant, seen
from April to October.
Prefers country, often near
water. Nests on rafters or
ledges in buildings. 19cm.

➡ House martin

Summer migrant. Builds
cup-shaped nest under
eaves. Found in town and
country. Catches insects
in flight. 13cm.

White
rump

White
underparts

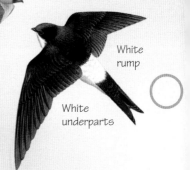

Brown back

Brown
band on
breast

⬅ Sand martin

Summer migrant. Groups
nest in holes in sandy cliffs
and other soft banks. Often
seen in flocks, catching
insects over water. 12cm.

Larks, pipits, dunnock

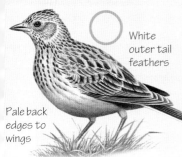

White outer tail feathers

Pale back edges to wings

← Skylark

Lives in open country, especially farmland. Rises to a great height, hovers, and sails down, singing. 18cm.

Orange outer tail feathers

→ Crested lark

Not often in Britain, but widespread in central and southern Europe. Open, often barren, areas. 17cm.

← Meadow pipit

Most common on upland moors, but also in fields, marshes and other open areas, especially in winter. 14.5cm.

→ Tree pipit

Summer migrant to heaths and places with scattered trees or bushes. Often perches on branches. 15cm.

← Dunnock

Common, even in gardens. Feeds under bird tables. Mouse-like walk. Often flicks wings. 14.5cm.

Wagtails

➡ **Pied wagtail**
➡ **White wagtail**

The white wagtail is widespread in Europe, but only the pied wagtail is usually seen in Britain. Common, even in towns. 18cm.

Pied wagtail

White wagtail

Juveniles of both kinds are grey

⬅ **Grey wagtail**

Usually nests near fast-flowing water in hilly areas. Paler yellow in winter, when it visits lowland waters. 18cm.

Male has black throat

Summer

♂

Blue-headed wagtail, central Europe

Yellow wagtail, Britain and Ireland

♂

♂

➡ **Blue-headed wagtail**
➡ **Yellow wagtail**

Two different forms of the same species. Summer visitor to grassy places near water. Yellow wagtail only seen in Britain. 17cm.

♂

Spanish wagtail, Spain and Portugal

♂

Ashy-headed wagtail, southern Europe

All the birds on this page wag their tails up and down

Waxwing, dipper, wren, shrikes

Resembles a starling in flight

← Waxwing
Rare winter visitor from northern Europe. Feeds on berries. May be seen in towns. 17cm.

Northern Europe

Britain and central Europe

→ Dipper
Fast-flowing rivers and streams in hilly areas. Bobs up and down on rocks in water. Walks underwater to find food. 18cm.

Flies fast and straight on tiny, rounded wings

← Wren
Very small. Found almost everywhere. Loud song finishes with a trill. Never still for long. 9.5cm.

♂ ♀

→ Red-backed shrike
Rare visitor to Britain. Catches and eats insects and small birds. 17cm.

Sticks food on thorns to store it

← Great grey shrike
Winter visitor to open country in Britain. Feeds on birds and mammals. Often hovers. 24cm.

Warblers

➡ Sedge warbler

Summer migrant. Nests in thick vegetation, usually near water, but also in drier areas. Sings from cover and is often difficult to see. 13cm.

White stripe over eye

Reddish-brown rump

⬅ Reed warbler

Summer visitor. Nests in reed beds or among waterside plants, mainly in the south of England. Hard to spot. Look for it flitting over reeds. 13cm.

➡ Garden warbler

Summer visitor. Sings from dense cover and is hard to see. Likes undergrowth or thick hedges. Song can be confused with blackcap's. 14cm.

Brown above, paler below

Female's cap is reddish-brown

♂

♀

⬅ Blackcap

Common summer visitor to woods or places with trees. Always moving from perch to perch as it sings. 14cm.

Male has grey head and white throat. Females and young have brown heads

◄ ## Whitethroat

A summer migrant, which hides itself in thick, low bushes. Sometimes sings its fast, scratchy song in flight. Flight is short and jerky. 14cm.

♂

➤ Willow warbler

Summer migrant. Most common British warbler. Its song, which comes down the scale, is the best way of telling it from the chiffchaff. 11cm.

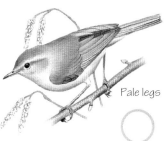

Pale legs

Dark legs

◄ Chiffchaff

Summer migrant, often arriving in March. A few spend the winter in Britain. Its repetitive "chiff-chaff" song can be heard in woods and from bushes. 11cm.

➤ Wood warbler

Summer migrant to open woods. Sings from a branch, repeating a note faster and faster until it becomes a trill. 13cm.

Yellow breast, white underparts

Flycatchers, chats

← Pied flycatcher

Catches insects in air. Also feeds on the ground. Summer migrant to old woodland. 13cm.

→ Whinchat

Summer migrant, found in open country. "Tic-tic" call. Perches on tops of bushes and posts. 13cm.

Flicks wings and tail

Colour is duller in winter

← Stonechat

"Tac-tac" call sounds like stones being knocked together. Found on heaths with gorse, especially near the sea. 13cm.

→ Wheatear

Summer migrant to moors and barren areas, but also seen elsewhere in the spring and autumn. 15cm.

White rump and black tail

➡ Spotted flycatcher

Summer migrant. Likes open woods, parks and country gardens. Catches insects in flight. 14cm.

Sits upright, often on a bare branch

♀

♂

⬅ Redstart

A summer migrant to open woods, heaths and parks. Constantly flickers its tail. 14cm.

♀

♂

➡ Black redstart

A few nest on buildings or on cliffs in Britain. Some winter in south of England. Flickers its tail. 14cm.

Male and female look alike

⬅ Robin

Woodland bird that is familiar in gardens. Sings in winter and spring. "Tic-tic" is its call of alarm. 14cm.

➡ Nightingale

Secretive summer migrant. Best found by listening for its song in May and June. 17cm.

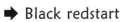

Reddish tail

Thrushes, oriole

➡ Fieldfare

Winter visitor, but a few nest in England and Scotland. Flocks can be seen in autumn, eating berries. 25.5cm.

⬅ Ring ouzel

Summer migrant to moors and mountains. Visits lower areas on migration. Shyer than blackbird. Loud piping call. 24cm.

Young are lighter and spottier than female

➡ Blackbird

Lives where there are trees and bushes, often in parks and gardens. Loud musical song. Clucking alarm call. 25cm.

⬅ Golden oriole

Rare summer migrant most often seen in woods of eastern England. Hard to see as it spends a lot of time in tree-tops. 24cm.

Thrushes, starling

◀ Redwing

Winter migrant, but a few nest in Scotland. Feeds on berries in hedges and hunts worms. 21cm.

White stripe over eye

➡ Song thrush

Found near or in trees or bushes. Well-known for the way it breaks open snail shells. Often in gardens. 23cm.

Smaller than mistle thrush

◀ Mistle thrush

Large thrush found in most parts of Britain. Seen on the ground in fields and on moors. 27cm.

White under wing

White outer tail feathers

Adult in winter

Juvenile

➡ Starling

A familiar garden bird. Often roosts in huge flocks. Mimics songs of other birds. 22cm.

Tits

➡ Long-tailed tit

Hedgerows and the edges of woods are good places to see groups of these tiny birds. 14cm.

Northern and eastern Europe

Britain and western Europe

⬅ Crested tit

Widespread in Europe but in Britain only found in a few Scottish pine woods, especially in the Spey Valley. 11cm.

➡ Coal tit

Likes conifer woods, but often seen in deciduous trees. Large white patch on back of head. 11cm.

⬅ Blue tit

Seen in woods and gardens. Often raises its blue cap to form a small crest. Young are less colourful. 11cm

➡ Marsh tit

A bird of decidous woods, like the willow tit (not illustrated). Rarely visits gardens. 11cm.

No pale patch on wings

174

Tit, nuthatch, crests, treecreeper

➡ Great tit

Largest tit. Lives in woodlands and gardens. Nests in holes in trees or will use nestboxes. 14cm.

Broad black band on breast

⬅ Nuthatch

Deciduous woods in England and Wales. Climbs up and down trees in a series of short hops. Very short tail. Nests in tree-holes. 14cm.

➡ Treecreeper

Usually seen in woods climbing up tree trunks and flying down again to search for food. Listen for high-pitched call. 13cm.

Firecrest

White stripe over eye

Goldcrest

⬅ Firecrest
⬅ Goldcrest

Smallest European birds. Goldcrests are found in woods, especially of pine, all over Britain. Firecrests are much rarer. 9cm.

Finches

➡ Chaffinch

Found in gardens and wherever there are trees and bushes. Often seen in flocks on farmland in winter. 15cm.

♀

♀

Male's head is brown in winter

♂

⬅ Brambling

Winter migrant from northern Europe. Flocks feed on grain and seeds. Likes fruit from beech trees. 15cm.

♀

♂

➡ Greenfinch

A frequent visitor to gardens, especially in winter. Likely to nest wherever there are trees and bushes. 15cm.

♀

♂

⬅ Siskin

A small finch which nests in conifers. It sometimes visits gardens in winter to feed on peanuts. 11cm.

← Bullfinch

Secretive bird often found on edges of woods, and in hedges or gardens. Eats seeds and also buds from fruit trees. 15cm.

White rump shows in flight

→ Linnet

Lives on heathland and farmland, but also found in towns, where it may visit gardens. Feeds on the seeds of weeds. Flocks in winter. 13cm.

← Lesser redpoll
← Common redpoll

The lesser redpoll is common in birch woods and forestry plantations in Britain. The common redpoll lives in northern Europe. 12cm.

Lesser redpoll

Common redpoll

→ Goldfinch

Feeds on thistle seeds and other weed seeds in open places. Nests in trees. 12cm.

Yellow wing bar

Crossbill, crows

♀ ♂

← Crossbill

Nests in pine woods. A slightly different species nests in Scotland. Eats pine cone seeds. 16cm.

Crossbills are sparrow-sized, with large heads and bills

➡ Jay

Secretive woodland bird. Will visit gardens. Listen for harsh screeching call. Look for white rump in flight. 32cm.

← Raven

This large crow lives in wild rocky areas or on rocky coasts. Look for its wedge-shaped tail and huge bill. Croaks. 64cm.

➡ Jackdaw

Small member of the crow family. Found where there are old trees, old buildings, or cliffs. Nests in colonies. Often seen with rooks. 33cm.

← Carrion crow
← Hooded crow

Carrion crow is more often seen alone or in pairs. Hooded crows form flocks. Carrion is more widespread than hooded. 47cm.

Carrion crow – England, Wales and southern Scotland

Hooded crow – northern Scotland and Ireland

➡ Rook

Nests in "rookeries" in tops of trees. Is usually seen in flocks on farmland. Young lack bare skin round beak. Call is harsh "kaw". 46cm.

Baggy thigh feathers

← Magpie

Seen in both town and country. Eats many eggs and young birds in spring. Long tail is very noticeable in flight. 46cm.

179

Pigeons, doves

➡ Woodpigeon

Largest of the pigeons. Common on farmland and in woods and towns. Forms large flocks. 41cm.

White on wings

Grey rump. No white on wings

⬅ Stock dove

Nests in holes in trees or in rock faces. Feeds on the ground, often with woodpigeons. Sometimes seen in flocks. 33cm.

➡ Rock dove
➡ Town pigeon

Town pigeons are descended from rock doves which are usually found in small groups on sea cliffs. 33cm.

Town pigeons   White rump

White on tail

⬅ Collared dove

Found in parks, large gardens, or near farm buildings. Feeds mainly on grain. 30cm.

➡ Turtle dove

Summer visitor to England and Wales. Woods, parks and farmland. Listen for purring call. 28cm.

White edge to tail

180

Sparrows, buntings

➡ House sparrow

Very familiar bird. Lives near houses and even in city centres, where it eats scraps. Often seen in flocks. 15cm.

♂ ♀

Brown cap and smudge below eye

Male and female look alike

⬅ Tree sparrow

Usually nests in holes in trees or cliffs. Much less common than house sparrow. 14cm.

➡ Yellowhammer

Found in open country, especially farmland. Feeds on ground. Forms flocks in winter. Sings from the tops of bushes. 17cm.

♀

♂ ♀

⬅ Reed bunting

Most common near water, but some nest in dry areas with long grass. May visit bird tables in winter. 15cm.

♀

♂

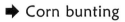

➡ Corn bunting

Nests in cornfields. Sings from posts, bushes or overhead wires. 18cm.

181

Bugs &
Insects

Butterflies

➡ Meadow brown

Meadows and grassy
places where it visits
thistles, knapweed
and bramble flowers.
Active even on dull days.
Caterpillar eats grasses.
W.S. 50-55mm.

Bramble

⬅ Ringlet

Keeps to damp, grassy
places and sunny
woodland paths.
Visits thistles,
knapweed and
bramble flowers.
W.S. 48-52mm.

Thistle

⬇ Small heath

Not fussy about where it
lives, and found in open
woods, on marshes
and on dry hillsides.
Likes hawkweed.
W.S. 33-35mm.

Hawkweed

➡ Gatekeeper or hedge brown

Basks in sunshine on roadside hedges, especially on bramble. Most common in the south. W.S. 40-46mm.

Butterflies fly around during the day, unlike moths, which are active at night.

Bramble

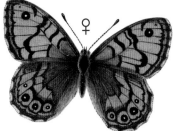

➡ Wall brown

Often rests on walls and paths. Likes rough, open ground and woodland glades. Flies slowly. Caterpillar eats grasses. W.S. 44-46mm.

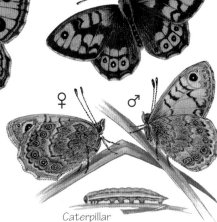

Caterpillar

Butterflies

Thistle

◀ Dark green fritillary

Likes thistle and bramble flowers. Open grassland near woods, and high rough ground. Flies fast. W.S. 63-70mm.

➡ Peacock

Common in gardens. One of five British species that hibernates in adult stage, in hollow trees, sheds, etc. Caterpillar eats nettles. W.S. 62-68mm.

The markings are like the "eyes" on a peacock's tail

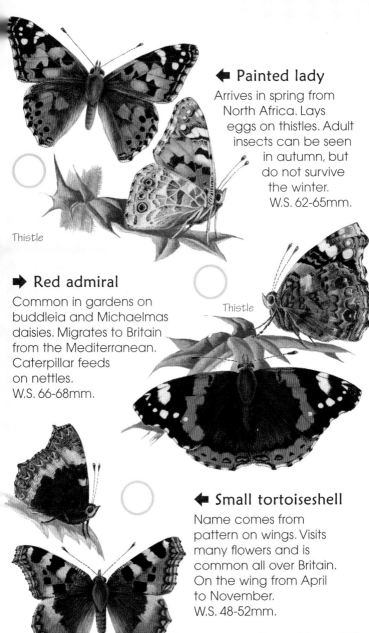

← Painted lady

Arrives in spring from North Africa. Lays eggs on thistles. Adult insects can be seen in autumn, but do not survive the winter.
W.S. 62-65mm.

Thistle

→ Red admiral

Common in gardens on buddleia and Michaelmas daisies. Migrates to Britain from the Mediterranean. Caterpillar feeds on nettles.
W.S. 66-68mm.

Thistle

← Small tortoiseshell

Name comes from pattern on wings. Visits many flowers and is common all over Britain. On the wing from April to November.
W.S. 48-52mm.

187

Butterflies

➡ Small white

Appears in May and
August. Lays single
eggs on cabbages
and nasturtiums.
Common in gardens.
W.S. 48-50mm.

◀ Green-veined white

Pattern on underwing
helps to protect the
butterfly from enemies
when it sits on grass.
Caterpillar eats leaves
and seed pods of
Jack-by-the-hedge.
W.S. 47-50mm.

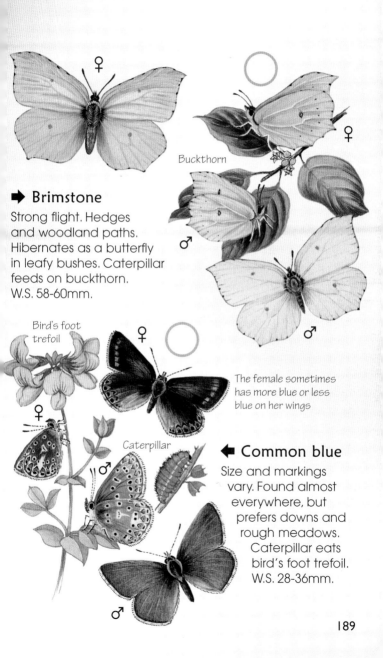

➡ Brimstone

Strong flight. Hedges and woodland paths. Hibernates as a butterfly in leafy bushes. Caterpillar feeds on buckthorn. W.S. 58-60mm.

Buckthorn

♀

♂

♂

Bird's foot trefoil

♀

♀

Caterpillar

♂

The female sometimes has more blue or less blue on her wings

⬅ Common blue

Size and markings vary. Found almost everywhere, but prefers downs and rough meadows. Caterpillar eats bird's foot trefoil. W.S. 28-36mm.

♂

Moths

Most moths are nocturnal, which means they are active at night. Moths' antennae don't have swellings at the ends like those of butterflies.

➡ Death's-head hawk

Occasionally visits Britain from southern Europe and northern Africa. Lays eggs on potato leaves. Larva is seen in late summer and pupates underground. W.S. 100-125mm.

Markings like a skull

Potato

⬅ Privet hawk

Most common in southern England and the Midlands. Larva eats privet leaves in July and August. Moth emerges the following summer. W.S. 90-100mm.

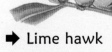

Privet

Lime

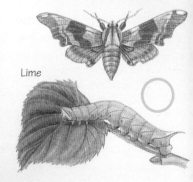

➡ Lime hawk

One of Britain's most common hawk moths. Larva eats leaves of lime trees in late summer. W.S. 65-70mm.

➡ Eyed hawk

Flashes markings on its underwings to frighten birds and other enemies. Larva feeds on sallow and leaves of plum and apple trees. W.S. 75-80mm.

Eye-like markings

Apple

Yellow points

Poplar

⬅ Poplar hawk

Common all over Britain. Larva feeds on poplar or willow and, like eyed hawk, has rough skin surface. Notice yellow markings. W.S. 75-80mm.

➡ Hummingbird hawk

Visitor to Britain. Found in gardens during day. Hovers over flowers to feed, beating its wings like a hummingbird. Lays eggs on bedstraw plants. W.S. 45mm.

Bedstraw

191

Moths

➡ Elephant hawk

Widespread, but scarce in Scotland. Larva is shaped like an elephant's trunk. It feeds on willowherb and bedstraw plants.
W.S. 65mm.

Willowherb

♀

♂

Sloe

⬅ Emperor

Found all over Britain. Male flies by day over moorland, looking for female which comes out at dusk. Lays eggs on heather and brambles. Appearance of larva changes each time its skin is shed. W.S. female 70mm. Male 55mm.

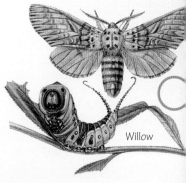

Willow

➡ Puss

Widespread in Britain. Lays eggs, usually singly, on willow in May-June. Thin red "whips" come out of larva's tails, perhaps to frighten birds. W.S. 65-80mm.

➡ Lobster

Can be seen in southern England, Wales and parts of southern Ireland. Name comes from the shape of the larva's tail end. Larva eats beech leaves. W.S. 65-70mm.

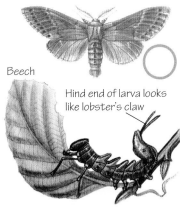

Beech

Hind end of larva looks like lobster's claw

♂

♀

Hawthorn

⬅ Vapourer

Common all over Britain, even in towns. Female has only wing stubs and can't fly. Larva feeds on a variety of trees. W.S. 35mm.

➡ Peach blossom

Found in woodland areas. Its name comes from the peach blossom pattern on its wings. Larva feeds on bramble. W.S. 35mm.

Peach blossom pattern

Bramble

Moths

Hawthorn

← Yellow-tail
Brightly coloured larvae are often found in hedgerows of hawthorn, sloe and bramble in May and June. W.S. 32-40mm.

Merveille-du-jour

Oak

➡ Merveille-du-jour
Lives in oak woodlands. Forewings match oak tree bark, making moth difficult for enemies to see. Larva eats oak leaves. W.S. 45mm.

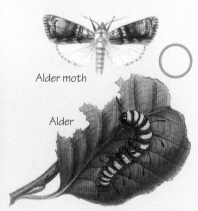

Alder moth

Alder

← Alder
Like many other species, the larva is more striking than the adult moth. It feeds on a variety of trees, including alder and oak. W.S. 37mm.

➡ Clifden nonpareil or blue underwing

Breeds in a few places in Kent, but sometimes visits other parts of Britain, usually in late summer. Stick-like larva feeds on black poplar and aspen.

Colour of upper wings matches tree bark

Larva of red underwing

Willow

⬅ Red underwing

Quite common in southern England and the Midlands. Flashes underwings when threatened by birds. Rests in daytime on trees. Larva eats poplar and willow. W.S. 80mm.

➡ Mother Shipton

Flies on sunny days. Look on railway banks and in meadows May to June. Larva eats vetches and clover. Named after a woman who was believed to be able to see into the future. W.S. 35mm.

Face-like marking on wings

Clover

Larva of Mother Shipton

Moths

Y-shaped markings

← Silver Y

Visitor to Britain, some years in great numbers. Feeds on garden flowers with long proboscis. Flies fast. Larva eats nettle and thistle. W.S. 40mm.

➡ Herald

Widespread in Britain. Hibernates during the winter in barns, sometimes in small groups. Mates in spring and female lays eggs on various kinds of willow. W.S. 40mm.

Larva of herald

Willow

♂

Female is larger and paler

← Oak eggar

Male flies by day, searching for female who rests in heather on moorland. Larva eats heather, bramble and hawthorn. W.S. 50-65mm.

Hawthorn

➡ Lappet

Name comes from "lappets" on larva. Feeds on apple, willow and hawthorn. Adult's brown colour, ragged wing edges and veined wings make it look like a bunch of leaves. W.S. 60-70mm.

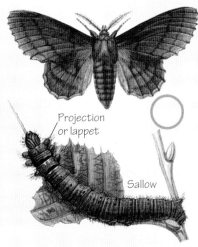

Projection or lappet

Sallow

Wing pattern varies

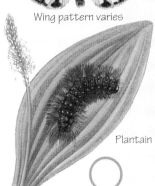

Plantain

➡ Garden tiger

Common, but larva more often seen. Feeds on many low-growing plants and hibernates when young. Feeds again in spring and is fully grown by June. W.S. 60-70mm.

⬅ Wood tiger

Smaller and more local than garden tiger. Widespread on hillsides, heaths and open woodland. Larva eats violets and forget-me-nots, and hibernates. W.S. 35-40mm.

Larva is called a woolly bear

Moths

➡ Cinnabar

Sometimes flies by day, but weakly. Striped larvae feed in groups on ragwort. Common on waste ground and railway banks. W.S. 40-45mm.

Ragwort

Larva inside tree trunk

⬅ Goat

Widespread, but well camouflaged and rarely seen. Larva eats wood of ash and willow. Spends three or four years in a tree trunk and pupates a silk-bonded cocoon made of wood shavings. Larva smells like goats. W.S. 70-85mm.

➡ Swallow-tailed

Looks like a butterfly. Weak, fluttering flight. Stick-like larva feeds on leaves of ivy, hawthorn and sloe. W.S. 56mm.

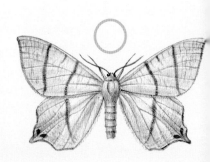

← Six-spot burnet

The most common British burnet. Flies over grassy areas during the day. Larva eats trefoil, clover and vetch. Boat-shaped cocoons are found attached to plant stems. W.S. 35mm.

♀

→ Ghost

Very common. Males often seen after dusk searching for larger females in dense grass. Female clings without moving to grass stem until male approaches. Larva eats plant roots. W.S. 50-60mm.

Female is better camouflaged than male

♂

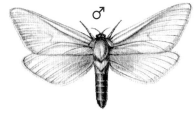

← Forester

Widely distributed. Flies over lush meadows. Stubby larva feeds on sorrel. W.S. 25-27mm.

199

Beetles

➤ Green tiger beetle

Fierce, sharp-jawed predator. Open woodland and sandy areas in early summer. Larva catches ants when they approach its burrow. 12-15mm long.

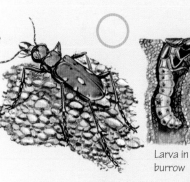

Larva in burrow

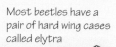

Most beetles have a pair of hard wing cases called elytra

◄ Large green ground beetle

Adults live in oak trees. Both adults and larvae feed on leaf-eating caterpillars and other larvae. 16-20mm long.

➤ Violet ground beetle

Found under large stones in gardens, and common in woods and under hedges. Adult and larva eat other insects and worms. Larva pupates in soil. 30-35mm long.

Gas from abdomen

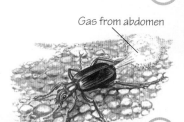

◄ Bombardier beetle

Lives under stones in chalky areas in southern England. When threatened, it shoots irritating gas from end of its abdomen with a popping sound. 7-10mm long.

200

Larva

← Devil's coach horse or cocktail beetle

Common in gardens. When challenged, raises tail and spreads jaws. Can ooze poisonous liquid from end of abdomen. 25-30mm long.

→ Rove beetle

Feeds mainly on dead animals and birds. Most common in southern England. Related to Devil's coach horse. 20mm long.

Mouse

← Red and black burying beetle

Feeds on dead animals, kneading and biting the flesh and then burying the body. Female lays eggs in burrow beside the body. Larvae feed on it and pupate in a chamber in soil. 15-20mm long.

→ Ant beetle

Small, fast-moving beetle found on elms and conifers. Larvae live under loose bark. Adults and larvae eat larvae of bark beetles. 7-10mm long.

Beetles

➡ Great diving beetle

Lives in lakes and large ponds. Eats tadpoles, small fish and other insects. Collects air from surface and stores it between wing covers and end of abdomen. 30-35mm long.

Male's wing cases are smoother than female's

♀

Larva

Carries bubble of air under body

⬅ Great silver water beetle

Largest British water beetle. Eats mainly water plants, but larva is a predator and eats water snails. Can fly to other waters if its home dries up. 37-48mm long.

➡ Whirligig beetle

Seen in groups on surface of ponds, lakes and slow rivers in bright sunshine. Darts in all directions. Carnivorous, eating mosquito larvae. 6-8mm long.

⬅ Water beetle

Lives under water, among vegetation of lakes and rivers, where it lays its eggs. Colour may be darker, sometimes all black. Widespread. 7-8mm long.

➡ Glow-worm

Likes grassy banks, hillsides, open woods. Most common in southern England. Wingless female attracts male with her glowing tail. Male 15mm long. Female 20mm long.

Larva

⬅ Lesser glow-worm

Seen near streams on damp grassy banks. Male and larva have small lights on tip of abdomen. Found in central and southern Europe, but not in Britain. 8-10mm long.

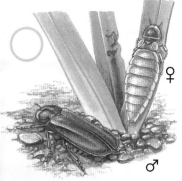

➡ Scarlet-tipped flower beetle

Most common in southern England. Look in buttercups and other flowerheads. Blows up scarlet bladders on its underside when handled. 7-10mm long.

Buttercup

⬅ Click beetle or skipjack

Found in dense vegetation or in flowers. Larvae live in soil, eating plant roots. Other species of click beetle do much damage to crops. 14-18mm long.

Larva is called a wireworm

Beetles

➡ Two-spot ladybird

Very common. Colour pattern often varies and some individuals are shiny black with red spots. 4-5mm long.

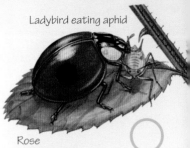

Ladybird eating aphid

Rose

⬅ Seven-spot ladybird

Very common. Hibernates in large numbers in sheds, houses or tree bark. Emerges on sunny spring days to find aphids and lay its eggs. 6-7mm long.

➡ Eyed ladybird

Largest ladybird in Britain. Found near or on fir trees. Both adults and larvae hunt for aphids. 8-9mm long.

22-spot ladybird

14-spot ladybird

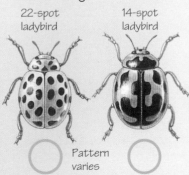

Pattern varies

⬅ 22-spot ladybird
⬅ 14-spot ladybird

22-spot is found in many areas and habitats. 2-3mm long. 14-spot is rare in the north. Likes trees and bushes. 3-4mm long.

➡ Death watch beetle

Larva eats timber in buildings. The sound the adult makes when it taps its head against its tunnel walls was once believed to foretell a death. 7-10mm long.

⬅ Cardinal beetle

Found on flowers and under bark. Whitish larvae feed on bark and wood. 15-17mm long.

➡ Oil beetle

This beetle cannot fly. The larva waits in a flower for a special kind of solitary bee to carry it to its nest where the larva feeds and grows. 15-30mm long.

⬅ Blister beetle

Rare. Name comes from a fluid in the insect's blood which causes blisters on human skin. Larvae live as parasites in the nests of some types of bee. 12-20mm long.

Beetles

➡ Stag beetle

Largest British beetle.
Only male has antlers.
Larvae feed on tree
stumps for three years
or more. Most common
in southern England.
25-27mm long.

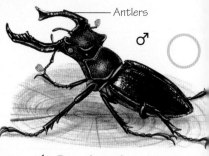

Antlers

♂

⬅ Dor beetle

Common. Seen flying
at night to dung heaps
where it lays its eggs.
Makes a loud droning
sound when it flies.
16-24mm long.

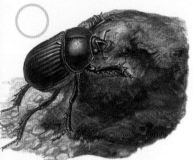

➡ Horned dung beetle or Minotaur beetle

Found in sandy places
where rabbits live. Eats
their dung and fills tunnels
with it for larvae to eat.
12-18mm long.

⬅ Cockchafer or May bug

Common. Flies round tree
tops in early summer and
sometimes down chimneys
and at lighted windows.
Larvae may be dug up in
gardens. 25-30mm long.

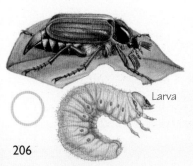

Larva

➡ Rose chafer

Sometimes found in roses and other flowers. Larvae feed on old timber and roots. Found all over Britain. 14-20mm long.

Rose

⬅ Bee beetle

Found mainly in Scotland and Wales. Found in flowers. Mimics colouring of bees (see page 39). Larvae eat rotting wood. 10-13mm long.

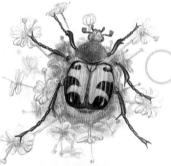

➡ Musk beetle

Longhorn beetles have long antennae, perhaps so they can recognize each other when they emerge from their pupae in wood tunnels. 20-32mm long.

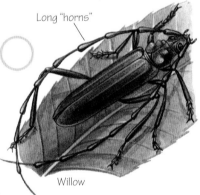

Long "horns"

Willow

⬅ Wasp beetle

Harmless, but looks and behaves like a wasp. Flies in bright sunshine visiting flowers. Common all over Britain. 15mm long.

207

Beetles

➤ Colorado beetle

Damages potato crops. Introduced by accident from America. Some still appear in Europe. You should tell the police if you spot one. 10-12mm long.

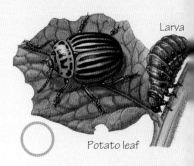

Larva

Potato leaf

⬅ Bloody-nosed beetle

Like oil beetle and blister beetle, it reacts when threatened, spurting bright red fluid from its mouth. This is called "reflex-bleeding". Found in low, dense foliage. 10-20mm long.

➤ Green tortoise beetle

Legs and antennae often hidden so it looks like a tortoise. Well camouflaged on thistles where it feeds, and where larvae pupate. 6-8mm long.

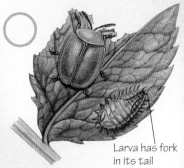

Larva has fork in its tail

⬅ Nut weevil

Female uses her long rostrum to pierce a young hazelnut, where she lays her single egg. Larva grows inside the nut, eating the kernel. 10mm long.

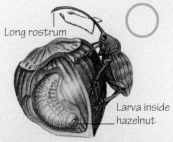

Long rostrum

Larva inside hazelnut

Bugs

➡ Green shieldbug

Lives on trees such as hazel and birch. Lays eggs in batches. Nymphs mature in late summer after several moults. 12-14mm long.

Birch

White dead-nettle plant

⬅ Pied shieldbug

Lays eggs in soil and female looks after them. When they hatch out, she leads the nymphs to their food plant. Rare in the north. 6-8mm long.

➡ Heath assassin bug

Common on open heath and sand dunes. Adults and nymphs suck body fluids out of prey. Most adults are wingless. 9-12mm long.

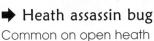

Oak

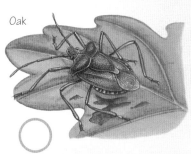

⬅ Forest bug

Common on oak or orchard trees. Feeds on leaves, fruits and caterpillars. Female lays batches of eggs on leaves. 11-14mm long.

Bugs

➡ Water cricket

Common on still and slow-moving water. Runs on water surface, eating insects and spiders. Lays eggs out of water on moss. 6-7mm long.

Breathing tube

⬅ Water scorpion

Found in ponds and shallow lakes. Seizes small fish, tadpoles and insect larvae with its forelegs. Lays eggs in algae or on water plants. 18-22mm long.

➡ Water stick insect

Not related to true stick insects, but like them it is hard to see among plants. Most common in southern Wales and southern England. 30-35mm long.

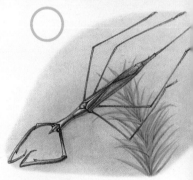

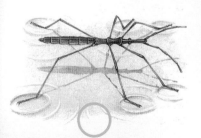

⬅ Water measurer

Found at edges of ponds and slow rivers and streams. Stabs at mosquito larvae and water fleas with its rostrum. Also eats dead insects. 9-12mm long.

➡ Water boatman or backswimmer

Lives in pools, canals, ditches and water tanks. Jerks along with its hind legs, usually on its back. Eats tadpoles and small fish. Can fly away if its home dries up. 15mm long.

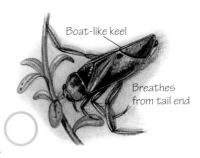

Boat-like keel

Breathes from tail end

⬅ Lesser water boatman

Flatter and rounder than water boatman, with shorter legs. It uses its front legs to swim. Sucks up bits of animal and plant material at bottom of ponds. Common. 12-14mm long.

➡ Pond skater

Front legs adapted to catch dead or dying insects that fall on water's surface. Some can fly; others have no wings. Common in ponds. 8-10mm long.

⬅ Saucer bug

Lives in vegetation at bottom of muddy pools and canals. Like the water boatman, it can stab with its rostrum. Hibernates in winter, as do most water bugs. 12-16mm long.

Bugs

➡ New Forest cicada

Male makes high-pitched buzzing sound that is very difficult to hear. Nymphs live underground for several years eating plant roots. The only British cicada. 25mm long.

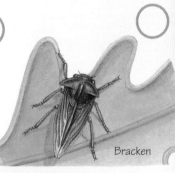

Adult sucks sap from trees

Birch

⬅ Southern cicada

Larger and noisier than British cicada. Common in southern Europe. Adult eats the sap of ash, pine and olive trees. 50mm long.

➡ Horned treehopper

Found on tree branches and low vegetation, such as bracken, in woods. Adult and larva feed on oak leaves and other plants. 9-10mm long.

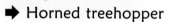

Bracken

⬅ Black and red froghopper

Common in dense grass and on trees. Jumps if disturbed. Larvae secrete froth which covers them when they feed underground. 9-10mm long.

➡ Eared leafhopper

Seen on lichen-covered oak or other trees where it is well hidden. Adults appear about June. Moves slowly. Local in southern England. 13-17mm long.

Ear-like projections

⬅ Green leafhopper

Common throughout Britain. Feeds on grasses and rushes in damp meadows and marshy places. 6-9mm long.

➡ Rose aphid or greenfly

Green or pinkish. Feeds on roses in spring, then moves to other plants. Excretes honeydew which ants feed on. Pest on roses. 2-3mm long.

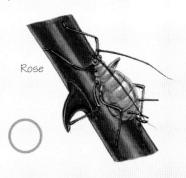

Rose

⬅ Bean aphid or blackfly

Common on broad bean, but also on thistle and other plants. Lays eggs on spindle trees. Adults produce fully formed young which eat beans. 2-3mm long.

213

Dragonflies and damselflies

➡ Downy emerald

This dragonfly flies fast and hovers over ponds, lakes and slow-moving streams and rivers in summer. Quite common in southern England. W.S. 68mm.

Female is longer than male

⬅ Golden-ringed dragonfly

Lives near streams and rivers, but like many dragonflies, it is sometimes seen far from water. Female lays eggs in mud. W.S. 100mm.

➡ Broad-bodied chaser

Seen over ponds and lakes with plenty of plants. Flies in short bursts. Most common in southern England. W.S. 75mm.

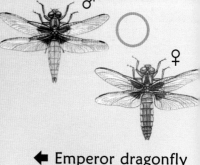

⬅ Emperor dragonfly

Seen over large ponds, lakes and canals in the summer. Adult catches flies in flight. W.S. 105mm.

Larva

➡ Ruddy darter

Found near weedy ponds or ditches in marshy areas. Nymphs mature more quickly than the larger dragonflies, which may take 2-3 years. W.S. 55mm.

♂

Female is duller colour than male

⬅ Beautiful demoiselle

Found near fast-flowing streams with sandy or stony bottoms. Damselflies usually rest with wings together, not spread out like dragonflies. W.S. 58-63mm.

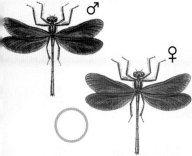

♂

♀

➡ Banded demoiselle

More common than the beautiful demoiselle, but rare in northern England and not recorded in Scotland. Usually seen by streams and rivers with muddy bottoms. W.S. 60-65mm.

♂

♀

⬅ Blue-tailed damselfly

Found on plants by ditches, canals, lakes, ponds and slow-moving rivers and streams. Common in most of Britain. W.S. 35mm.

♂

Bees, wasps, ants

Some bees, wasps and ants are solitary creatures.
Others are "social insects", living in colonies. These
colonies include queens, drones and workers.

➡ Red-tailed bumblebee

Common in gardens.
The queen makes a nest
in a hole in the ground.
Eggs develop into colonies
of queens, workers and
drones. Queen 22mm long.

Nest

⬅ Leaf-cutter bee

Cuts pieces from rose
leaves to make cylinders
where female lays an
egg. Solitary species.
Male 10mm long.
Female 11mm.

Leaves
cut by bee

➡ Potter wasp

Makes clay pots for its larvae.
Each one has a separate
pot, stocked with smaller
caterpillars (paralysed with
a sting) for food. Sandy
heaths. Male 12mm long.
Female 14mm.

Pot

⬅ Sand wasp

Makes a nest burrow in
sand where it lays a single
egg on top of a paralysed
caterpillar. Larva eats the
caterpillar. 28-30mm long.

➡ Ruby-tailed wasp

Also called a cuckoo-wasp because female lays egg in nest of a solitary bee or wasp. When larva hatches it eats its host's food and its egg or larva. 12mm long.

♀

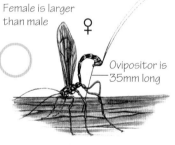

⬅ Velvet ant

Actually a wasp, but female is wingless. She lays her egg in a bee larva which is eaten by her own larva when it hatches. Can sting painfully. 15mm long.

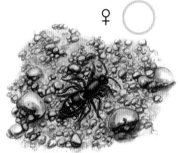

➡ Ichneumon wasp

Female pierces pine trees with her ovipositor (egg layer) and lays an egg on a horntail larva or in its burrow inside the tree. 22-30mm long.

Female is larger than male

♀

Ovipositor is 35mm long

⬅ Giant wood wasp or horntail

Female lays eggs in sickly or felled conifers. Larvae feed on wood for up to three years. 25-32mm long.

♂

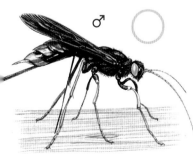

Wasps

➡ Blue horntail

Male is like male horntail except his head, thorax and the first two segments of his abdomen are deep metallic blue. Female is all blue and has only a short ovipositor. 20-25mm long.

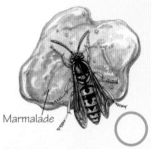

Ovipositor

Dog rose

⬅ Hornet

Not as likely to sting as the German wasp. Nests in hollow trees, banks or roofs. Preys on soft-bodied insects which it feeds to its larvae. Also feeds from flowers in woods. 22-30mm long.

➡ German wasp

One of the most common British species. Most likely to sting in late summer when larvae are mature. 15-20mm long.

Marmalade

⬅ Tree wasp

Likes to nest in woods, often hanging its oval nest from a tree branch. More locally distributed than German wasps. 15-20mm long.

Wasp's nest in tree

Ants

➡ Carpenter ant

Hollows out pine tree trunks where it nests, often making the tree fall down. Not in Britain. 8-18mm long.

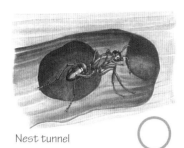
Nest tunnel

⬅ Wood ant

Makes large conical nest from twigs and leaves in pine woods. Useful to foresters as it eats leaf-eating larvae. Cannot sting, but sprays formic acid at intruders. 5-11mm long.

Nest

➡ Red ant

Nests under stones or in rotting wood. Rears aphids in its nest and feeds on the sugary liquid they produce. 3-6mm long.

Nest in tree stump

⬅ Black ant

Common in gardens. Like all ants, only queens and males have wings. Males die after mating and queens start a new colony. 3-9mm long.

Ant, sawfly, gall-wasps

➡ Yellow meadow ant

Makes small mounds in meadows. Sometimes "farms" other small insects, such as aphids, for a sugary liquid that they produce. 2-9mm long.

⬅ Birch sawfly

Name "sawfly" comes from female's saw-like ovipositor. Larva feeds on birch leaves in late summer. It makes a large oval cocoon and the adult emerges the next spring. 20-23mm long.

Sawfly larva has nine pairs of legs

➡ Oak marble gall-wasp

Female lays egg in a leaf bud. Larva's feeding causes the tree to "blister" around it. Only one larva lives in each "marble". 4mm long.

Marble gall

⬅ Oak apple gall-wasp

These galls can be 40mm across and are at first red and green and then later darken. Each gall contains many larvae. Insect is 3mm long.

Oak apple gall

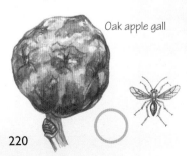

True flies

True flies have only one pair of wings. The second pair are replaced by two "halteres", which are like tiny drumsticks. Flies probably use them for balance. The insects that appear on pages 224-226 are not true flies.

➡ Grey flesh fly

Common. Lays eggs in carrion. White, legless larvae (known as maggots) feed on flesh before turning into oval brown pupae. 6-17mm.

Rat

⬅ Greenbottle fly

Most species lay eggs in carrion. Adults seen on flowers. One species lays eggs in skin or fleece of sheep. Its larvae eat the sheep's flesh. 7-11mm long.

➡ Drone fly

Makes a loud, bee-like droning in flight. Visits flowers for nectar and pollen. Larva rests on pond bottom and breathes through a long tube. 15mm long.

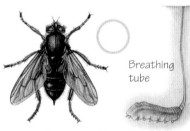

Breathing tube

⬅ Hover fly

Hovers as though motionless. Common in summer. Female lays eggs among aphids and the legless larvae eat them. 10-14mm long.

Antirrhinum flower

221

True flies

➡ Dung fly

Visits fresh cowpats where female lays eggs. Many rise in a buzzing mass if disturbed, but soon settle again. Larvae eat dung but adults are predators on other flies. 10-12mm long.

Cowpat

⬅ Robber fly

Preys on other insects by capturing them and sucking out their body fluids. Larvae feed on animal dung as well as vegetable matter. 18-26mm long.

Robber fly killing damsel fly

➡ Bee fly

Probes flowers in gardens for nectar in spring. Lays eggs near bees' nests and its larvae eat the bees' larvae. Most common in southern England. 10-11mm long.

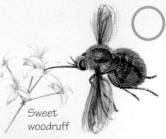

Sweet woodruff

⬅ Horse fly

Female sucks blood, but her loud hum warns you before you get bitten. Smaller species are more silent and stab before being noticed. Found in old forests in southern England. 20-25mm long.

A horse fly piercing someone's arm

➡ Fever fly

Does not bite or cause fever. Most noticeable in spring and summer. Males perform courtship dance in the air above females. 8mm long.

Water violet

⬅ Giant cranefly or daddy-long-legs

Often found near water. Other species found in gardens where larvae (called leatherjackets) eat root crops and grass roots. 30-40mm long.

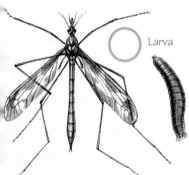
Larva

➡ Black and yellow cranefly

Found in low vegetation. Craneflies mate end to end and can be seen joined like this in summer. Female lays eggs in soil with her pointed ovipositor. 18-20mm long.

⬅ Common gnat or mosquito

Female sucks people's blood. Lays eggs in clusters which float on water. Larvae hang down below surface. 6-7mm long.

Water surface

223

Ant-lion, lacewings

➡ Ant-lion

Name refers to larva which traps ants and other insects in a sandy hollow. Grabs them in its sickle-like jaws and sucks them dry. Not in Britain. Adult 35mm long.

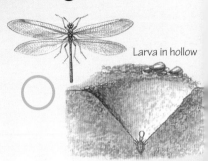

Larva in hollow

⬅ Giant lacewing

Mainly nocturnal. Larvae eat small midge larvae they find in wet moss at the water's edge. Pupates in yellowish, silken cocoons. 15mm long.

➡ Green lacewing

Found in gardens and hedges and sometimes attracted to house lights. Weak fluttering flight. Larvae feed on aphids. 15mm long.

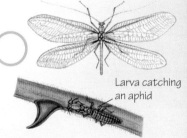

Larva catching an aphid

⬅ Brown lacewing

Smaller than green lacewing, with dark brownish transparent wings. Look near water in lush vegetation and on trees. Throughout Britain. 10mm long.

Scorpion fly, alder fly, snake fly

➡ Scorpion fly

Name comes from the scorpion-like shape of male's tail. Both adults and larvae eat dead insects and waste matter. 18-22mm long.

♂

♀

Notice shape of tail

⬅ Alder fly

Slow, heavy flier. Lays eggs on stems of water plants. Larvae live on water bottom where they eat small animals. 20mm long.

Egg mat

➡ Snake fly

Name comes from long head and thorax, which can bend, making the insect look like a cobra snake. 15-20mm long.

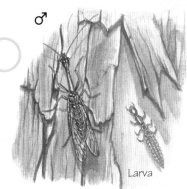

♂

Larva

Caddis fly, stonefly, Mayfly

➡ Caddis fly

Found near lakes and slow rivers. Many caddis larvae make a protective case from bits of twigs and tiny shells. 15-20mm long.

Caddis larva in case made of leaves

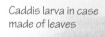

Wings overlap

⬅ Stonefly

Found mainly in fast-flowing rivers. Larvae live at river bottom feeding on other small animals. 22mm long.

Long tails

Larva on river bottom

➡ Mayfly

Adults live for a short time, perhaps only a few hours. In this time they mate and female lays her eggs in river water. 40mm long.

Long tails

Crickets

Crickets and bush crickets have very long antennae, while grasshoppers' are short. The third pair of legs on these insects is adapted for leaping. Males "sing" to attract females by rubbing their wing-cases together.

➡ Field cricket

Very rare. Lives in grassy banks and meadows in sandy or chalky areas. Male sings to attract female. 20mm long.

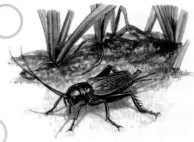

⬅ House cricket

Found in heated buildings and greenhouses, garden rubbish heaps and bigger tips. Rarely flies. Shrill song. 16mm long.

➡ Mole cricket

Burrows like a mole with its large spade-like forefeet. Lives in damp meadows. Male has a whirring call. Rare. 38-42mm long.

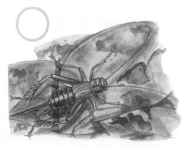

⬅ Wood cricket

Found in dead leaves in ditches and banks in southern England. Male has quiet, churring song. Flightless. 8-9mm long.

Grasshopper, bush crickets

Wings look silvery in flight

← Large marsh grasshopper

Found in bog and fenland in southern England, Norfolk Broads and Ireland. Flies a long way when disturbed. Male makes slow ticking sound. 27-32mm long.

→ Great green bush cricket

Harsh, shrill, penetrating song. Moves slowly and never flies far. Eats small insects found in dense vegetation. 45-47mm long.

Long hind legs

← Speckled bush cricket

Flightless adults seen in late summer or early autumn. Found in old gardens where shrubs grow. Male's song is hard to hear. 11-13mm long.

→ Wart-biter

May bite when handled. Some people used to use it to bite their warts off. Seen in coarse grassland on downs. Preys on small insects. 34-35mm long.

Cockroaches, mantis

➡ Common cockroach

Found in houses and other warm buildings, where it eats waste. Female lays eggs in purse-like containers. Does not fly. 25mm long.

Old bread

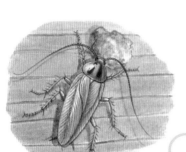

⬅ German cockroach

Not from Germany – it probably originated in northern Africa or the Middle East. Lives in heated buildings. 13mm long.

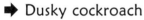

➡ Dusky cockroach

Lives out-of-doors, unlike its larger relatives. Found mainly in woodlands on leaves of trees. 7-10mm long.

⬅ Praying mantis

Holds its forelegs together, as if praying, while waiting for its insect prey to come close. Found in scrub and tall grass in southern Europe. Not in Britain. 60-80mm long

Stick insect, earwigs

➡ Stick insect

Lives in bushes in southern Europe. Eats vegetation. Another species is commonly kept as a pet. Not found in Britain. Up to 90mm long.

Forceps (see below) are spread and raised over body when earwig is threatened

♀   ♂

➡ Lesser earwig

Flies during the day, but is rarely noticed because it is small. Not rare, but less common than common earwig. 10mm long.

⬅ Common earwig

Eats small insects (usually dead), as well as leaves and fruits. Female guards nymphs until they can look after themselves. 15mm long.

Some other small insects

The insects on these pages are mostly very small and the pictures are greatly enlarged. The sizes given are very approximate.

← Water springtail

Lives on the surface of ponds and lakes. Can make spectacular jumps by flicking its tail (usually folded beneath its body). About 2mm long.

➡ Fleas

Many different species. Wingless, but can jump powerfully. Feed on blood of many mammals and birds. Closely related to flies. Average length is 2mm.

← Termites

Like ants, termites are social insects with queens, soldiers and workers. Live in colonies in rotting wood. Not found in Britain. Average length is 10-15mm.

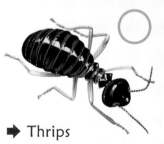

➡ Thrips

Tiny insects. Often settle on arms in hot summers and tickle. They are known as "thunder flies" because they are associated with thundery weather. About 1-2mm long.

Scorecard

When you start spotting, you'll soon find that some plants and animals are rarer than others. To give you a rough idea of how likely you are to see them, all the flowers, trees, birds and insects in the book are listed here with a score next to each one.

Common species score 5 points; rare ones are worth 25. Species are listed alphabetically. Where this book gives an alternative name, look up the first name that appears. If you want to, you can use the "Date spotted" boxes to record when you saw each species.

Species	Score	Date spotted	Species	Score	Date spotted
14-spot ladybird	15		Barberry	15	
22-spot ladybird	10		Barnacle goose	15	
Alder fly	5		Barn owl	20	
Alder moth	20		Bar-tailed godwit	15	
Aleppo pine	25		Bats-in-the-belfry	15	
Alpine rock cress	20		Bean aphid	5	
Alternate-leaved golden saxifrage	15		Bean goose	25	
Annual seablite	15		Beautiful demoiselle	15	
Ant beetle	15		Bee beetle	20	
Ant-lion	25		Bee fly	10	
Arctic tern	20		Bell heather	15	
Arrowhead	15		Bewick's swan	20	
Aspen	15		Bilberry	10	
Atlas cedar	10		Birch sawfly	10	
Avocet	20		Bird cherry	10	
Banded demoiselle	15		Bird's foot trefoil	10	

Species	Score	Date spotted	Species	Score	Date spotted
Bistort	10		Bombardier beetle	15	
Black and red froghopper	10		Brambling	20	
Black and yellow cranefly	10		Brent goose	20	
Black ant	5		Brimstone butterfly	10	
Blackberry	5		Broad-bodied chaser	10	
Blackbird	5	9/2/11	Broad-leaved pondweed	10	
Blackcap	15		Brooklime	10	
Black grouse	20		Brown lacewing	10	
Black-headed gull	5		Buckshorn plantain	5	
Black Italian poplar	10		Bugle	10	
Black mulberry	25		Bullfinch	15	
Black nightshade	10		Buzzard	15	
Black redstart	25		Caddis fly	10	
Black-tailed godwit	20		Canada goose	5	
Black tern	25		Canadian pondweed	10	
Blackthorn	5		Capercaillie	25	
Black woodpecker	25		Cardinal beetle	10	
Bladder campion	5		Carpenter ant	25	
Blister beetle	25		Carrion crow	5	
Blood-red geranium	10		Cedar of Lebanon	10	
Bloody-nosed beetle	15		Chaffinch	5	
Bluebell	10		Chickweed	5	
Blue-headed wagtail	25		Chiffchaff	10	
Blue horntail	15		Chile pine	10	
Blue-tailed damselfly	5		Chough	25	
Blue tit	5	6/2/11	Cinnabar moth	10	

Species	Score	Date spotted	Species	Score	Date spotted
Click beetle	15		Common St. John's wort	10	
Clifden nonpareil	25		Common sandpiper	15	
Coal tit	10		Common speedwell	10	
Coast redwood	20		Common tern	15	
Cockchafer	5		Common walnut	15	
Collared dove	5		Coot	10	
Colorado beetle	25		Cork oak	25	
Common alder	5		Corky-fruited water dropwort	25	
Common ash	5		Cormorant	10	
Common beech	5		Corn bunting	15	
Common blue butterfly	5		Corncrake	25	
Common centaury	10		Cornflower	25	
Common cockroach	5		Corn spurrey	10	
Common dog violet	10		Corsican pine	10	
Common earwig	5		Cow parsley	5	
Common forget-me-not	10		Cowslip	10	
Common fumitory	10		Crab apple	10	
Common gnat	5		Crack willow	10	
Common gull	15		Creeping buttercup	5	
Common lime	10		Creeping cinquefoil	5	
Common meadow rue	15		Creeping Jenny	15	
Common monkshood	20		Crested lark	25	
Common olive	25		Crested tit	20	
Common orache	5		Crossbill	20	
Common pear	20		Cuckoo	10	
Common redpoll	25		Curlew	15	

Species	Score	Date spotted	Species	Score	Date spotted
Cypress spurge	15		Emperor dragonfly	10	
Daisy	5		Emperor moth	15	
Dandelion	5		English elm	15	
Dark green fritillary butterfly	10		English oak	5	
Dawn redwood	25		European fan palm	25	
Death's-head hawk moth	25		European larch	10	
Death watch beetle	25		European silver fir	15	
Deodar cedar	5		Eyed hawk moth	10	
Deptford pink	25		Eyed ladybird	20	
Devil's bit scabious	10		False acacia	10	
Devil's coach horse	10		Fever fly	5	
Dipper	15		Field cricket	25	
Dog rose	15		Fieldfare	10	
Dog's mercury	10		Field maple	15	
Dor beetle	10		Field mouse-ear chickweed	15	
Douglas fir	10		Field scabious	10	
Downy emerald dragonfly	20		Firecrest	25	
Drone fly	10		Flea	5	
Dung fly	5		Floating water plantain	15	
Dunlin	10		Forest bug	10	
Dunnock	5		Forester moth	20	
Dusky cockroach	15		Foxglove	10	
Eared leafhopper	20		Fritillary	20	
Early purple orchid	15		Frogbit	15	
Eider	15		Fulmar	10	
Elephant hawk moth	15		Furze	10	

Species	Score	Date spotted	Species	Score	Date spotted
Gannet	15		Grand fir	15	
Garden tiger moth	10		Great black-backed gull	15	
Garden warbler	15		Great crested grebe	10	
Gatekeeper butterfly	10		Great diving beetle	10	
German cockroach	10		Greater bindweed	10	
German wasp	5		Greater plantain	5	
Ghost moth	10		Greater stitchwort	5	
Giant cranefly	10		Great green bush cricket	15	
Giant lacewing	15		Great grey shrike	25	
Giant wood wasp	20		Great silver water beetle	20	8/3/10
Glow-worm	25		Great spotted woodpecker	10	
Goat moth	20		Great tit	5	
Goat willow	5		Greek fir	20	
Goldcrest	10		Greenbottle fly	5	
Golden eagle	25		Greenfinch	20	
Goldeneye	15		Green lacewing	10	
Golden oriole	15		Green leafhopper	10	
Golden plover	25		Greenshank	15	
Golden-ringed dragonfly	10		Green shieldbug	10	
Golden rod	10		Green tiger beetle	10	
Golden samphire	10		Green tortoise beetle	10	
Goldfinch	10		Green-veined white butterfly	5	
Good King Henry	5		Green woodpecker	10	
Goosander	20		Grey alder	15	
Goosegrass	5		Grey flesh fly	5	
Goshawk	25		Grey heron	10	

Species	Score	Date spotted	Species	Score	Date spotted
Greylag goose	10		Horse fly	15	
Grey partridge	10		House cricket	15	
Grey wagtail	15		Houseleek	15	
Guillemot	15		House martin	10	
Hawthorn	5		House sparrow	5	
Heath assassin bug	10		Hover fly	10	
Heather	5		Hummingbird hawk moth	15	
Hedge parsley	15		Ichneumon wasp	10	
Hemp agrimony	10		Italian cypress	20	
Herald moth	10		Ivy-leaved toadflax	5	
Herb Bennet	10		Jack-by-the-hedge	5	
Herb Robert	10		Jackdaw	10	
Herring gull	5		Japanese larch	15	
Hoary plantain	5		Japanese red cedar	15	
Hobby	20		Jay	10	
Hogweed	10		Juniper	15	
Holly	5		Kestrel	10	
Holm oak	10		Kingfisher	15	
Honey buzzard	25		Knapweed	10	
Hooded crow	10		Knot	15	
Hoopoe	25		Knotgrass	5	
Hornbeam	10		Laburnum	5	
Horned dung beetle	15		Lappet moth	15	
Horned treehopper	15		Lapwing	10	
Hornet	20		Large green ground beetle	20	
Horse chestnut	5		Large marsh grasshopper	20	

Species	Score	Date spotted	Species	Score	Date spotted
Larkspur	15		Magnolia	15	
Lawson cypress	5		Magpie	5	6/2/11
Leaf-cutter bee	15		Maidenhair tree	20	
Lesser black-backed gull	10		Mallard	5	
Lesser celandine	5		Manna ash	20	
Lesser duckweed	5		Mare's tail	15	
Lesser earwig	15		Maritime pine	15	
Lesser glow-worm	25		Marram grass	10	
Lesser periwinkle	15		Marsh tit	15	
Lesser redpoll	20		Mayfly	10	
Lesser spotted woodpecker	20		Meadow brown butterfly	5	
Lesser water boatman	5		Meadow clary	20	
Leyland cypress	5		Meadow pipit	10	
Lily-of-the-valley	15		Meadow saxifrage	20	
Lime hawk moth	10		Meadowsweet	10	
Linnet	10		Merveille-du-jour moth	15	
Little grebe	15		Mistle thrush	10	
Little owl	15		Mole cricket	25	
Little ringed plover	20		Monterey cypress	15	
Little tern	20		Monterey pine	15	
Lobster moth	15		Moorhen	5	
Lombardy poplar	10		Mother Shipton moth	10	
London plane	5		Musk beetle	15	
Long-eared owl	25		Mute swan	5	
Long-headed poppy	5		Nettle	10	
Long-tailed tit	10		New Forest cicada	25	

Species	Score	Date spotted	Species	Score	Date spotted
Nightingale	15		Pigweed	10	
Nightjar	20		Pink-footed goose	20	
Noble fir	10		Pintail	20	
Nootka cypress	20		Pochard	15	
Norway maple	5		Policeman's helmet	15	
Norway spruce	5		Pond skater	5	
Nuthatch	15		Poplar hawk moth	10	
Nut weevil	5		Poppy	10	
Oak apple gall-wasp	5		Potter wasp	15	
Oak eggar moth	15		Praying mantis	25	
Oak marble gall-wasp	5		Primrose	10	
Oil beetle	15		Privet hawk moth	15	
Osprey	20		Ptarmigan	20	
Ox-eye daisy	10		Puffin	20	
Oystercatcher	15		Purslane	15	
Painted lady butterfly	15		Puss moth	10	
Pasque flower	25		Pygmy owl	25	
Peach blossom moth	10		Ragged Robin	15	
Peacock butterfly	10		Ramsons	15	
Pellitory-of-the-wall	15		Rape	5	
Peregrine	20		Raven	15	
Pheasant	5		Razorbill	15	
Pheasant's eye	25		Red admiral butterfly	10	
Pied flycatcher	20		Red and black burying beetle	10	
Pied shieldbug	10		Red ant	10	
Pied wagtail	10		Red-backed shrike	25	

Species	Score	Date spotted	Species	Score	Date spotted
Red-breasted merganser	20		Rowan	5	
Red campion	10		Ruby-tailed wasp	10	
Red grouse	15		Ruddy darter	10	
Red helleborine	25		Ruff	20	
Red kite	20		Sanderling	20	
Red-legged partridge	10		Sand martin	15	
Red oak	10		Sand spurrey	10	
Redshank	10		Sand wasp	10	
Redstart	15		Saucer bug	10	
Red-tailed bumblebee	5		Scarlet pimpernel	10	
Red underwing moth	15		Scarlet-tipped flower beetle	10	
Redwing	10		Scops owl	25	
Reed bunting	15		Scorpion fly	10	
Reed warbler	15		Scots pine	5	
Ribwort plantain	5		Sea arrowgrass	10	
Ringed plover	15		Sea aster	10	
Ringlet butterfly	10		Sea bindweed	4	
Ring ouzel	20		Sea campion	5	
Robber fly	15		Sea holly	15	
Robin	5		Sea kale	20	
Rock dove	25		Sea lavender	10	
Rook	10		Sea mayweed	10	
Rose aphid	5		Sea milkwort	10	
Rosebay willowherb	5		Sea purslane	10	
Rose chafer	15		Sea sandwort	10	
Rove beetle	5		Sea wormwood	10	

Species	Score	Date spotted	Species	Score	Date spotted
Sedge warbler	15		Song thrush	10	
Sessile oak	10		Sorrel	5	
Seven-spot ladybird	5		Southern beech	20	
Shag	15		Southern cicada	25	
Sheep's sorrel	15		Spanish fir	20	
Shelduck	15		Sparrowhawk	10	
Shepherd's purse	5		Speckled bush cricket	10	
Shore pine	10		Spiked water milfoil	10	
Short-eared owl	20		Spotted flycatcher	15	
Shoveler	15		Stag beetle	20	
Silver birch	5		Starling	5	
Silver lime	20		Starry saxifrage	15	
Silverweed	10		Stick insect	25	
Silver Y moth	5		Stock dove	15	
Siskin	15		Stonechat	15	
Sitka spruce	10		Stonecrop	10	
Six-spot burnet moth	10		Stonefly	10	
Skylark	10		Stone pine	25	
Small heath butterfly	5		Stonewort	20	
Small tortoiseshell butterfly	5		Summer pheasant's eye	25	
Small white butterfly	5		Swallow	10	
Snake fly	15		Swallow-tailed moth	10	
Snapdragon	5		Swamp cypress	25	
Snipe	15		Sweet chestnut	10	
Snowdrop	15	Sr	Sweet William	20	
Soapwort	20		Swift	10	

Species	Score	Date spotted	Species	Score	Date spotted
Swiss stone pine	25		Velvet ant	15	
Sycamore	5		Violet ground beetle	5	
Tamarisk	15		Viper's bugloss	10	
Tawny owl	15		Wall brown butterfly	15	
Teal	15		Wart-biter	25	
Tengmalm's owl	25		Wasp beetle	10	
Termites	20		Water beetle	10	
Thrift	5		Water boatman	5	
Thrips	5		Water cricket	15	
Touch-me-not balsam	25		Water crowfoot	10	
Town pigeon	5		Water forget-me-not	5	
Treecreeper	15		Water measurer	10	
Tree of Heaven	20		Water rail	20	
Tree pipit	20		Water scorpion	10	
Tree sparrow	20		Water soldier	25	
Tree wasp	10		Water springtail	15	
Triangular-stalked garlic	20		Water starwort	10	
Tufted duck	10		Water stick insect	15	
Tufted vetch	10		Water violet	20	
Tulip tree	20		Waxwing	20	
Turkey oak	10		Wellingtonia	10	
Turnstone	15		Western balsam poplar	10	
Turtle dove	15		Western hemlock	10	
Two-spot ladybird	5		Western red cedar	10	
Vapourer moth	10		Wheatear	15	

Species	Score	Date spotted	Species	Score	Date spotted
Whimbrel	20		Willow warbler	10	
Whinchat	15		Woad	20	
Whirligig beetle	5		Wood anemone	10	
Whitebeam	10		Wood ant	10	
White bryony	15		Woodcock	20	
White campion	10		Wood cricket	15	
White clover	5		Wood groundsel	15	
White dead-nettle	5		Woodpigeon	5	8/2/11
White-fronted goose	20		Wood sorrel	5	
White poplar	10		Wood tiger moth	15	
White stork	25		Wood warbler	20	
Whitethroat	15		Wood woundwort	10	
White wagtail	25		Wren	5	
White water-lily	15		Wych elm	15	
White willow	5		Yarrow	5	
Whooper swan	20		Yellow archangel	10	
Wigeon	15		Yellowhammer	10	
Wild carrot	10		Yellow horned poppy	15	
Wild chamomile	15		Yellow meadow ant	5	
Wild cherry	5		Yellow pimpernel	10	
Wild pansy	10		Yellow-tail moth	5	
Wild pea	20		Yellow wagtail	15	
Wild strawberry	15		Yellow water-lily	10	
Willow grouse	25		Yew	5	

Useful words

These pages explain some specialist words you might come across when reading about flowers, trees, birds and insects. Words that are written in *italic* text are defined separately.

abdomen – the rear section of an insect, attached to the *thorax*

air bladders – pockets filled with air, which help some water plants to float

algae – tiny water plants

annual ring – a ring of dark and light wood in the cross-section of a *trunk* or branch that shows one year's growth

antenna (plural: **antennae**) – a pair of feelers on an insect's head used for feeling and smelling

anther – the top part of the *stamen*. It produces *pollen*.

bar – a natural mark across a feather or group of feathers

bark – a tough outer layer that protects the tree's insides

belly – part of a bird's body between its *breast* and tail

bill – another word for beak

bird of prey – a bird such as an eagle which hunts other animals for food

blossom – flowers

bract – (1) a leaf-like structure at the base of a *flower* or stalk (2) a leaf-like part of a *cone* supporting the seed

breast – part of a bird's body between its throat and *belly*

breeding season – the time of year when a pair of birds builds a nest, mates, lays eggs and looks after its young. In Britain this is usually spring.

broadleaved tree (**broadleaf**) – a tree that has wide, flat leaves. Most broadleaved trees are *deciduous*.

bud – an undeveloped *shoot*, leaf or *flower*

bud scale scar – a ring-shaped mark around a twig, left when the *scales* of the *terminal bud* fall off

bulb – a mass of thick, fleshy leaves which store food for a plant under the ground

calyx – a name for all the *sepals* together

cambium – a thin layer that produces new *inner bark* and *sapwood* in a tree *trunk*

camouflage – when an animal's colour makes it difficult to see against certain backgrounds

carnivores – animals that feed on other animals

carpel – the female part of the *flower*. It consists of the *stigma*, *style* and *ovary*.

carrion – the flesh of a dead animal

castes – different physical forms in *colonies* which have different functions

catkin – an often sausage-shaped cluster of tiny *flowers*, all of the same sex, growing on one stalk

chlorophyll – a green chemical found in leaves that absorbs sunlight to help make food for the plant

chrysalis – see *pupa*

cocoon – a case which protects an insect *pupa*, made by the *larva* before it pupates

colony – a group of birds, insects or other animals of the same *species* that live close together

compound eye – an eye made up of many lenses

compound leaf – a type of leaf made up of smaller *leaflets*

cones – the fruits of *conifers*

conifer – a tree with needle-like or scaly leaves, which bears *cones* with their *seeds* inside. Most are *evergreen*.

corolla – all a *flower's petals*

cover – anywhere that animals hide themselves, for example hedges, bushes or thick grass

crown – (1) the collective name given to a tree's branches, twigs and leaves (2) the top part of a bird's head

cutting – a part of a tree, such as a *shoot* or *root*, cut off and used to grow a new tree

deciduous – losing its leaves over a few weeks, usually in autumn

display – courtship behaviour to attract and keep a mate

drone – male *social insect*

entire leaf – a leaf that has a smooth edge

entomology – the study of insects

estuary – the place where a large river meets the sea; a river mouth. Fresh water is mixed with sea water and at low tide large areas of mud are exposed.

evergreen – losing its leaves throughout the year, so the plant is always green

excrete – to get rid of waste from the body

eyrie – the nest of a bird of prey. The term is generally used for the large nests of eagles.

fertilization – the joining of an *ovule* with *pollen* to make a *seed*

filament – the stalk of the *stamen*. It supports the *anther*.

fleshy – plump, thick (used to describe leaves)

flock – a group of birds of the same *species* feeding or travelling together

flowerhead – a cluster of small *flowers*. It often looks like a single flower.

flowers – the parts of a plant where new *seeds* are made

foliage – all the leaves of a tree

food plant – a plant that an insect *species* feeds on

fruits – the parts of a plant that hold its *seeds*

game bird – a bird such as a pheasant of partridge that is hunted by humans for food or sport

habitat – the place where a plant or animal *species* lives

heartwood – old wood at the core of the *trunk* that has grown too solid to carry water

herbivores – animals that feed on plants

hibernation – a sleepy state in which some animals survive winter

honeydew – a sweet liquid *excreted* by some insects

host – a plant or animal that is attacked by a *parasite*

hover – when a bird or insect stays in one place in the air by flapping its wings very fast

immature – a young bird which has grown out of its juvenile *plumage* but is not yet in adult plumage

inner bark – a layer beneath the outer layer of *bark* that grows every year

irruptions – irregular journeys from the usual pattern of *migration*

juvenile – a young bird that does not yet have full, adult *plumage*

larva (plural: **larvae**) – the young stage of an insect which is very different from the adult insect

leaflets – leaf-like sections that make up a *compound leaf*

leaf scar – mark left on a twig where a leaf has fallen off

leaf skeleton – the dried-up remainder of a leaf

lek – an area where the male birds of some *species* gather to perform a courtship *display* to females

lobed leaf – a type of leaf or *leaflet*, partly divided into sections called lobes

local – plants and animals that are found only in certain areas

mandibles – the biting, piercing and cutting mouthparts of an insect

marsh – an area of low-lying land which gets flooded either by a river or the sea

metamorphosis – the process of changing from an egg to an adult, via a *larva* and (often) a *pupa*

migrant – a bird that breeds in one area, then moves to another for the winter, returning again the following spring

migration – a regular movement of birds from one place to another, from the breeding area to the area where they spend the winter. Migrating birds are called *migrants* or visitors.

mimicry – when an animal's shape or colour copies that of another *species*, sometimes of a different *order*, often to put off predators

moult – (1) the shedding of an insect's skin to allow growth (2) when birds lose their old feathers and grow new ones. All birds do this at least once a year.

nape – the back of a bird's neck

nectar – a sweet, sticky liquid produced by some plants to attract insects

nocturnal – active at night

nymph – a young insect which looks like a miniature adult, and acquires wings during growth

offshore – out at sea, some way from a shore

omnivores – creatures that feed on plants and animals

order – one of the scientific divisions of animals

ovary – a female part of a *flower* that contains *ovules*

ovipositor – a female insect's egg-laying organ

ovule – a plant "egg"

parasite – a living thing that feeds off another plant or animal without killing it

partial migrant – when some members of a *species* are migrant while others are resident

perch – (1) when a bird stands on a branch or other resting place by gripping with its toes (2) the place where a bird perches

petal – a segment of the *corolla*, usually brightly coloured

plumage – all the feathers on a bird

pollen – a powder made by the flower's male parts for transfer to the female parts to make *seeds*

pollination – when *pollen* reaches the *stigma*

predator – an animal that kills and eats other animals

prey – an animal that is hunted by another animal for food

primaries – a bird's large, outer wing feathers

proboscis – a long, tube-like tongue of some insects

pupa (plural: **pupae**) – the stage after the *larval* stage, during which the adult insect develops

queen – a female *social insect* which lays eggs

resident – a bird that can be seen throughout the year

roost – (1) when a bird sleeps (2) a place where birds sleep

rootlet – the smallest of a plant's *roots*

roots – parts of a plant that grow into the ground, absorbing water and goodness from the soil and anchoring the plant

rostrum – the long, tube-like stabbing mouthpart of bugs and weevils

rump – the area of a bird's body above its tail

runner – a stem that grows along the ground

saltmarsh – a marsh which gets flooded by sea water

sand dunes – a mound or ridge of loose sand formed by the wind

sap – a liquid that carries sugars (food made in the leaves) around a plant

sapwood – the outer area of wood in a tree *trunk* that carries water up from the roots to the rest of the tree

scales – (1) the tough, woody parts of a *cone* (2) a *bud's* outer layers

scavenger – an animal that feeds on waste and dead matter

secondaries – a bird's inner wing feathers

secrete – when an animal's body produces and gives off a chemical from a gland

seed – grows from a fertilized *ovule*, and may eventually form a new plant

seedling – a very young plant that has grown from a *seed*

sepals – leaf or *petal*-like growths which protect the flower *bud* and support the *flower* once it opens

shingle – (1) pebbles that have been rounded and worn to roughly the same small size by the sea (2) a beach which is made up of these pebbles

shoot – a young stem or twig bearing leaves

simple leaf – a type of leaf that is all in one piece

social insects – insects that live in *colonies* and are organized so that each of the *castes* has different duties to keep the colony running smoothly

species – a group of plants or animals that all look alike, behave in the same way and can breed together

spine – (1) a stiff, sharp-pointed outgrowth on a plant or animal (2) a prickle

spur – a tube formed by the *petals* of some flowers. It often contains *nectar*.

stamen – the male part of a *flower*, where *pollen* is made. Each stamen is made up of an *anther* and a *filament*.

stigma – the top part of the *carpel*. It receives the *pollen* when the flower is *pollinated*.

stoop – a Peregrine's dramatic dive at its prey

style – part of the *carpel* which joins the *stigma* to the *ovary*

tendril – a thin stem or leaf that helps a plant to climb

terminal bud – a *bud* at the tip of a *shoot* or twig

territory – the area defended by an animal, or a pair of animals, for breeding

thorax – the middle section of an insect to which the legs and wings are attached

timber – wood, especially when harvested

toothed leaf – a leaf or *leaflet* with jagged edges

trunk – the main woody stem of the tree that holds it upright

tuber – a large, underground stem

variegated – a type of leaf that has two or more colours

veins – tiny tubes inside a leaf that carry water to all parts of the leaf and carry food away from it

wader – one of a group of long-legged birds that live near water and often wade in search of food

weed – a plant that grows on waste or cultivated land, often getting in the way of other plants

worker – female *social insect* that cannot breed. These insects work for the *colony*.

Index

acacia, false 131
agrimony, hemp 60
alder, common 114
    grey 114
amaranth, common see pigweed
anemone, wood 69
ant, black 219
    carpenter 219
    red 219
    velvet 217
    wood 219
    yellow meadow 220
ant-lion 224
aphid, bean 213
    rose 213
apple, crab 122
archangel, yellow 45
arrowgrass, sea 88
arrowhead 83
ash, common 113
    manna 113
aspen 116
aster, sea 88
auks 154
avens, wood see herb Bennet
avocet 151
backswimmer see water boatman
bacon and eggs see trefoil, bird's foot
balsam, touch-me-not 63
barberry 44
bats-in-the-belfry 63
bee, leaf-cutter 216
beech, common 121
    southern 120
beetle, ant 201
    bee 207
    blister 205
    bloody-nosed 208
    bombardier 200
    cardinal 205
    click 203
    cocktail see beetle, Devil's
        coach horse
    Colorado 208
    death watch 205
    Devil's coach horse 201
    dor 206
    great diving 202
    great silver water 202
    green tiger 200
    green tortoise 208
    horned dung 206

beetle (cont'd)
    large green ground 200
    Minotaur see beetle, horned dung
    musk 207
    oil 205
    red and black burying 201
    rove 201
    scarlet-tipped flower 203
    stag 206
    violet ground 200
    wasp 207
    water 202
    whirligig 202
bilberry 58
bindweed, greater 55
    sea 87
birch, silver 118
birds of prey 155-159
bistort 55
blackberry 54
blackbird 172
blackcap 168
blackfly see aphid, bean
blackthorn 123
bluebell 53
bluebottle see cornflower
blue, common 189
blue underwing see Clifden nonpareil
bramble see blackberry
brambling 176
brimstone 189
brooklime 52
brown, meadow 184
    wall 185
bryony, white 71
bug, forest 209
    heath assassin 209
    saucer 211
bugle 52
bugloss, viper's 51
bullfinch 177
bumblebee, red-tailed 216
bunting, corn 181
    reed 181
buttercup, creeping 42
butterflies see individual species names
buzzard 157
    honey 155
campion, bladder 76
    red 61
    sea 89
    white 76

capercaillie 161
carrot, wild 72
cedar, Atlas 108
    deodar 109
    Japanese red 105
    of Lebanon 108
    western red 102
celandine, lesser 42
centaury, common 59
chafer, rose 207
chaffinch 176
chamomile, wild 79
chaser, broad-bodied 214
chats 170
cherry, bird 129
    wild 129
chestnut, horse 128
    sweet 128
chickweed 77
    field mouse-ear 73
chiffchaff 169
chough 145
cicada, New Forest 212
    southern 212
cinquefoil, creeping 46
clary, meadow 53
cleaver, common see goosegrass
clover, white or Dutch 73
cockchafer 206
cockroach, common 229
    dusky 229
    German 229
cocks and hens see plantain, ribwort
coot 144
cormorant 145
corncrake 144
cornflower 50
cowslip 43
cranefly, black and yellow 223
    giant 223
cranesbill, bloody see geranium,
        blood-red
creeping Jenny 43
cress, Alpine rock 80
cricket, field 227
    great green bush 228
    house 227
    mole 227
    speckled bush 228
    water 210
    wood 227
crossbill 178
crow, carrion 179
    hooded 179
cuckoo 159
curlew 149

cypress, Italian 103
    Lawson 102
    Leyland 104
    Monterey 103
    Nootka 98
    swamp 104
dabchick see grebe, little
daddy-long-legs see cranefly, giant
daisy 73
    ox-eye 79
damselfly, blue-tailed 215
dandelion 47
darter, ruddy 215
dead-nettle, white 75
demoiselle, banded 215
    beautiful 215
dipper 167
dove, collared 180
    rock 180
    stock 180
    turtle 180
downy emerald 214
dragonfly, emperor 214
    golden-ringed 214
dropwort, corky-fruited water 72
duck, tufted 141
ducks 140-143
duckweed, lesser 83
dunlin 150
dunnock 165
eagle, golden 156
earwig, common 230
    lesser 230
eider 141
elm, English 127
    wych 127
fieldfare 172
finches 176-177
fir, Douglas 101
    European silver 98
    grand 100
    Greek 99
    noble 100
    Spanish 99
firecrest 175
fireweed see willowherb, rosebay
flea 231
fly, alder 225
    bee 222
    caddis 226
    drone 221
    dung 222
    fever 223
    greenbottle 221
    grey flesh 221
    horse 222

fly (cont'd)
  hover 221
  robber 222
  scorpion 225
  snake 225
flycatcher, pied 170
  spotted 171
forget-me-not, common 51
  water 53
foxglove 63
fritillary (flower) 64
fritillary, dark green (butterfly) 186
frogbit 82
froghopper, black and red 212
fulmar 154
fumitory, common 56
furze 46
gall-wasp, oak apple 220
  oak marble 220
game birds 160-161
gannet 145
garlic, triangular-stalked 81
  wood see ramsons
gatekeeper 185
geese 138-139
geranium, blood-red 61
giant sequoia see Wellingtonia
glow-worm 203
  lesser 203
gnat, common 223
godwit, bar-tailed 149
  black-tailed 148
goldcrest 175
goldeneye 142
golden rod 48
goldfinch 177
Good King Henry 75
goosander 142
goose, barnacle 138
  bean 139
  Brent 138
  Canada 138
  greylag 138
  pink-footed 139
  white-fronted 139
goosegrass 77
gorse see furze
goshawk 155
Granny's nightcap see
  anemone, wood
grasshopper, large marsh 228
grebe, great crested 143
  little 143
greenfinch 176
greenfly see aphid, rose
greenshank 148

groundsel, wood 45
grouse, black 160
  red 160
  willow 160
guillemot 154
gull, black-headed 152
  common 152
  great black-backed 152
  herring 153
  lesser black-backed 152
gulls 152-153
hard-head see knapweed
hawthorn 123
heartsease see pansy, wild
heather 58
  bell 58
heath, small 184
hedge brown see gatekeeper
helleborine, red 54
hemlock, western 101
herb Bennet 44
herb Robert 57
heron, grey 143
hobby 155
hogweed 72
holly (tree) 132
  sea 87
hoopoe 162
hornbeam 121
hornet 218
horntail see wasp, giant wood
  blue 218
houseleek 65
hyacinth, wild see bluebell
Jack-by-the-hedge 70
jackdaw 178
jay 178
jumping Jack see policeman's helmet
juniper 105
keck see hogweed
kestrel 157
kingfisher 162
kite, red 156
knapweed 60
knot 150
knotgrass 56
laburnum 131
lacewing, brown 224
  giant 224
  green 224
ladybird, 14-spot 204
  22-spot 204
  eyed 204
  seven-spot 204
  two-spot 204
Lady's lace see parsley, cow

lapwing 146
larch, European 97
   Japanese 97
lark, crested 165
larkspur 50
lavender, sea 88
leafhopper, eared 213
   green 213
leek, three-cornered see
    garlic, triangular-stalked
lily-of-the-valley 68
lime, common 126
   silver 126
ling see heather
linnet 177
magnolia 135
magpie 179
maidenhair tree 134
mallard 140
mantis, praying 229
maple, field 125
   Norway 125
mare's tail 85
marguerite see daisy, ox-eye
marram grass 87
martin, house 164
   sand 164
May bug see cockchafer
Mayfly 226
mayweed, scented see
    chamomile, wild
   sea 89
meadow rue, common 43
meadowsweet 81
mercury, dog's 68
merganser, red-breasted 142
milfoil, spiked water 84
milkwort, sea 88
monkey puzzle see Chile pine
monkshood, common 52
moorhen 144
mosquito see gnat, common
moth, alder 194
   cinnabar 198
   Clifden nonpareil 195
   death's-head hawk 190
   elephant hawk 192
   emperor 192
   eyed hawk 191
   forester 199
   garden tiger 197
   ghost 199
   goat 198
   herald 196
   hummingbird hawk 191
   lappet 197

moth (cont'd)
   lime hawk 190
   lobster 193
   merveille-du-jour 194
   Mother Shipton 195
   oak eggar 196
   peach blossom 193
   poplar hawk 191
   privet hawk 190
   puss 192
   red underwing 195
   silver Y 196
   six-spot burnet 199
   swallow-tailed 198
   vapourer 193
   wood tiger 197
   yellow-tail 194
mulberry, black 130
mustard, garlic see Jack-by-the-hedge
nettle 74
nightingale 171
nightjar 162
nightshade, black 77
nuthatch 175
oak, cork 112
   English 110
   holm 111
   red 112
   sessile 110
   Turkey 111
olive, common 133
orache, common 74
orchid, early purple 62
oriole, golden 172
osprey 156
owl, barn 158
   little 158
   long-eared 159
   pygmy 158
   Scops 159
   short-eared 159
   tawny 158
   Tengmalm's 159
oystercatcher 146
painted lady 187
palm, European fan 133
pansy, wild 49
parsley, cow 71
   hedge 71
partridge, grey 161
   red-legged 161
Pasque flower 64
peacock 186
pear, common 122
pea, wild 70
pellitory-of-the-wall 80

peregrine 155
periwinkle, lesser 50
pheasant 161
pheasant's eye 67
   summer 67
pigeon, town 180
   woodpigeon 180
pigweed 74
pimpernel, scarlet 66
   yellow 44
pine, Aleppo 94
   Chile 109
   Corsican 94
   maritime 92
   Monterey 95
   Scots 92
   shore 93
   stone 93
   Swiss stone 95
pink, Deptford 61
   sea see thrift
pintail 140
pipit, meadow 165
   tree 165
plane, London 124
plantain, buckshorn 89
   floating water 81
   greater 78
   hoary 78
   ribwort 78
plover, golden 147
   little ringed 147
   ringed 147
pochard 141
policeman's helmet 62
pond skater 211
pondweed, broad-leaved 83
   Canadian 84
poplar, black Italian 116
   Lombardy 118
   western balsam 117
   white 117
poppy 66
   long-headed 66
   yellow horned 86
primrose 45
ptarmigan 160
puffin 154
purslane 48
   sea 87
ragged Robin 60
rail, water 144
ramsons 69
rape 49
ratstails see plantain, greater
raven 178

razorbill 154
red admiral 187
redpoll, common 177
redpoll, lesser 177
redshank 148
redstart 171
   black 171
redwing 173
redwood, coast 107
   dawn 106
ringlet 184
ring ouzel 172
robin 171
rook 179
rose, dog 55
rowan 115
ruff 150
sage, meadow see clary, meadow
St. John's wort, common 47
samphire, golden 86
sanderling 150
sandpiper, common 148
sandwort, sea 86
sawfly, birch 220
saxifrage, alternate-leaved golden 42
   meadow 80
   starry 80
scabious, Devil's bit 64
   field 64
seablite, annual 88
sea kale 86
sea pink see thrift
shag 145
shelduck 142
shepherd's purse 75
shieldbug, green 209
   pied 209
shoveler 141
shrike, great grey 167
   red-backed 167
silverweed 46
siskin 176
skipjack see beetle, click
skylark 165
snake's head see fritillary
snakeweed see bistort
snapdragon 65
snipe 151
snowdrop 69
soapwort 56
sorrel 59
   sheep's 59
   wood 54
sparrowhawk 157
sparrow, house 181
   tree 181

speedwell, common 51
springtail, water 231
spruce, Norway 96
   Sitka 96
spurge, cypress 49
spurrey, corn 76
   sand 57
starling 173
starwort, water 85
stick insect 230
   water 210
stitchwort, greater 68
stonechat 170
stonecrop 48
stonefly 226
stonewort 85
stork, white 143
strawberry, wild 70
swallow 164
swan, Bewick's 139
   mute 139
   whooper 139
sweet William 67
swift 164
sycamore 124
tamarisk 132
teal 140
termites 231
tern, Arctic 153
   black 153
   common 153
   little 153
thrift 89
thrips 231
thrush, mistle 173
   song 173
tit, blue 174
   coal 174
   crested 174
   great 175
   long-tailed 174
   marsh 174
toadflax, ivy-leaved 65
tortoiseshell, small 187
treecreeper 175
treehopper, horned 212
tree of Heaven 135
trefoil, bird's foot 46
tulip tree 134
turnstone 146
vetch, tufted 62
violet, common dog 63
   water 84
waders 146-151
wagtail, blue-headed 166
   grey 166
   pied 166

wagtail (cont'd)
   white 166
   yellow 167
wallpepper see stonecrop
walnut, common 130
warbler, garden 168
   reed 168
   sedge 168
   willow 169
   wood 169
wart-biter 228
wasp, German 218
   giant wood 217
   ichneumon 217
   potter 216
   ruby-tailed 217
   sand 216
   tree 218
water boatman 211
   lesser 211
water crowfoot 82
water-lily, white 83
   yellow 83
water measurer 210
water scorpion 210
water soldier 82
waxwing 167
weasel-snout see archangel, yellow
weevil, nut 208
Wellingtonia 107
wheatear 170
whimbrel 149
whin see furze
whinchat 170
whitebeam 115
white, green-veined 188
   small 188
whitethroat 169
wigeon 140
willow, crack 119
   goat 119
   white 120
willowherb, rosebay 57
woad 47
wolfsbane see monkshood, common
woodcock 151
woodpecker, black 163
   great spotted 163
   green 163
   lesser spotted 163
woodpigeon 180
wormwood, sea 87
woundwort, wood 67
wren 167
yarrow 79
yellowhammer 181
yew 106

Acknowledgements

Edited by Felicity Brooks, Jane Chisholm, Jessica Datta,
Rosie Dickins, Sue Jacquemier, Kirsteen Rogers, Ingrid Selberg,
Sue Tarsky, Philippa Wingate

Designed by Cristina Adami, Reuben Barrance, Nicola Butler, Nayera Everall,
Laura Fearn, Joanne Kirkby, Lucy Owen, Susannah Owen and Andrea Slane
with thanks to Zöe Wray and Lucy Parris

Cover designer: Michael Hill

Digital manipulation by Mike Olley

Additional illustrations
Joyce Bee, Kuo Kang Chen, Victoria Goaman, Ian Jackson,
Aziz Khan, Michelle Ross, Chris Shields

Photo credits
Every effort has been made to trace the copyright holders of the material in
this book. If any rights have been omitted, the publishers offer their sincere
apologies and will rectify this in any subsequent editions following notification.
The publishers are grateful to the following organizations for their
contribution and permission to reproduce material.
Cover: © Alan Williams/Alamy (wagtail) © Westend61/Alamy (leaves)
© Joe Mamer Photography/Alamy (trees) © Jupiter Images/ Brand X/
Alamy (flowers); 1 © D. Hurst/Alamy; 2-3 © blickwinkel /Alamy ;
4-5 © Chris Gomersall /naturepl.com; 12 © Stockbyte; 14-15 © Landlife;
30-31 © James Marshall/Corbis; 34-35 © Denise Swanson /Science Photo
Library; 37 © Ralph A. Clevenger/Corbis; 40-41 © Pal Hermansen/Stone/
Getty Images; 90-91 © Martin Ruegner/Photographer's Choice/Getty
Images; 136-137 © Steve Knell/naturepl.com; 182-183 © Richard Cummins/
Corbis (butterfly) © Aflo Foto Agency /Alamy (daisies)

This edition first published in 2008 by Usborne Publishing Ltd.,
Usborne House, 83-85 Saffron Hill, London
EC1N 8RT, England. www.usborne.com